QUILTING FOR BEGINNERS

THE ULTIMATE GUIDE TO MASTER
THE ART OF QUILTING, WITH PRACTICAL STEP-BY-STEP
INSTRUCTIONS AND EASY PROJECT IDEAS.

HAIDEE GLENN

Copyright - Haidee Glenn - 2020 -

All rights reserved.

The content contained within this book may not be reproduced, duplicated or transmitted without direct written permission from the author or the publisher.

Under no circumstances will any blame or legal responsibility be held against the publisher, or author, for any damages, reparation, or monetary loss due to the information contained within this book. Either directly or indirectly.

Legal Notice:

This book is copyright protected. This book is only for personal use. You cannot amend, distribute, sell, use, quote or paraphrase any part, or the content within this book, without the consent of the author or publisher.

Disclaimer Notice:

Please note the information contained within this document is for educational and entertainment purposes only. All effort has been executed to present accurate, up to date, and reliable, complete information. No warranties of any kind are declared or implied. Readers acknowledge that the author is not engaging in the rendering of legal, financial, medical or professional advice. The content within this book has been derived from various sources. Please consult a licensed professional before attempting any techniques outlined in this book.

By reading this document, the reader agrees that under no circumstances is the author responsible for any losses, direct or indirect, which are incurred as a result of the use of information contained within this document, including, but not limited to, - errors, omissions, or inaccuracies.

TABLE OF CONTENTS

INTRODUCTION ... 7

CHAPTER 1
What is Quilting? ... 9

THE HISTORY OF QUILTING ... 9

CHAPTER 2
Quilting Tools To Get Started ... 13

SEAM RIPPER ... 13
THIMBLES ... 13
PATTERNS OR TEMPLATES ... 14
PENCILS OR FABRIC MARKERS ... 15
BRASS SAFETY PINS ... 15
LONG QUILTING PINS, SILK PINS ... 15
PIN CUSHION ... 16
IRON ... 16
QUILTING FABRICS ... 16
TYPES OF FABRICS FOR QUILTING ... 16
TIPS FOR CHOOSING THE RIGHT FABRICS ... 17
FABRIC MARKERS ... 19
QUILTING HOOPS AND FRAMES ... 19
CUTTERS ... 19
SHEARS OR SCISSORS ... 19
QUILTING MACHINES ... 20
CROCHET HOOK, BODKIN, TOOTHPICK OR COCKTAIL STICK ... 20
BATTING ... 20
NEEDLES ... 21

CHAPTER 3
Anatomy of a Quilt ... 23

BATTING ... 23
TOP ... 24

BLOCK	24
THE DESIGN	24
THE SIZE OF THE QUILT	25
BUILDING THE BLOCKS	25
SASHING	27
QUILTING	27
BINDING	27
CORNERSTONES	27
BACKING	27
QUILT SANDWICH	29

CHAPTER 4
The Different Types of Quilts — 31

WHOLE CLOTH	32
SCRAP QUILTS	32
PATCHWORK OR PIECED QUILT	32
APPLIQUÉ QUILT	33
ART QUILTS AND WALL HANGINGS	34
AMISH QUILTS	35
BLOCK QUILT	35
MODERN QUILTS	36

CHAPTER 5
Quilting Techniques — 37

PAPER PIERCING	37
TYING	37
STITCH-AND-FLIP FOUNDATION PIECING	37
FOUNDATION FABRIC	38
PIECING METHOD	39
APPLIQUÉ	40
STITCHING IN THE DITCH	40
HAND QUILTING	41
MACHINE QUILTING	41

CHAPTER 6
Basic Care and Laundering — 43

SHOULD YOU PRE-WASH YOUR FABRIC?	43
PROS TO PREWASHING:	44
CONS TO PRE WASHING:	44
PERFORMING A BLEEDING TEST	45

PREVENTING THE FABRIC FROM FRAYING 46

CHAPTER 7
Step By Step Quilt Projects 47

GARDEN PILLOW 47
SIMPLE BABY BLUSH 54
MODERN GRANNY MINI QUILT/PILLOW 56
ARROW TABLE RUNNER 61
PILLOW PINCUSHION 64
CHAIN OF DIAMONDS 69
PILLOW SHAM 76
WINDOW GARDEN MINI QUILT 82
POSY PATCH MINI QUILT 88
GIANT HEXIE FLOWER LAP QUILT 92
STAR BABY QUILT 94
SIMPLY WOVEN QUILT 96
DONUTS (THE SIZE OF YOUR HEAD) 100
SCRAP HAPPY RAILS 107
GARDEN SCENES QUILT 111

CONCLUSION 119

INTRODUCTION

Welcome to the world of quilting!

Quilting is a relaxing hobby that can be started by anyone who wants a creative way to spend their time. It can help a person create pleasant and artistic pieces that can be of practical use. There are many things you can do once you enter the world of quilting You can add color and design to your home or create unique quilts to give as a precious gift to friends and family.

Quilting might seem like an intimidating hobby. You can approach this new hobby through many different angles. There are many things to learn if you are just trying out quilting for the first time. So, you just need to find a starting point that you are comfortable with.

Naturally, you shouldn't start with a complicated project. A basic quilting pattern of a mini quilt is a good starting point. Once you get the basics of construction, composition, and stitching, you can move on to more complicated projects. Before you know it, you can create patchwork pillows, silhouette quilts, and wall hangings. Your home will honestly look more beautiful if you have these homemade decorations that will give any space a personalized and unique touch.

Quilts are as much a part of American history and tradition as having a turkey for Thanksgiving dinner is. It holds a central role in the life of every American family, serving as both a practical piece of bedding material and as a receptacle that holds the memories of important family events.

The quilt itself is not the only part of the tradition that matters. The process of creating the quilt also plays a central role in the aesthetic and sentimental value of the end-product.

But beyond its importance as a heritage craft, research shows that quilting has unique health benefits. A study conducted by a team of researchers at the University of Glasgow discovered that quilting improves not only a person's creativity, but also enhances individual wellbeing in many ways that outdoor and physical activities could not.

The researchers studied quilters and concluded that this hobby helped their emotional, creative, and cognitive well-being, especially among older individuals.

Quilting plays an essential role in social self-growth, as it increases the self-confidence of the individual. It also harnesses the mind with math and geometric challenges and could elevate the mood of the individual by using different colors. Stress has also been found to decrease overall activity.

Hence, it is an excellent decision to start quilting, and I am happy that you have chosen this book to be your guide in discovering the wonders of this beautiful hobby.

In this book, I will teach you the most essential things you must know before you can start quilting. No, you do not need any previous quilting experience to start. We will start with a bit of history, we will then discover the most common quilting tools and fabrics, learning how to pick and choose them, and what types of fabrics to avoid.

We will then talk about the anatomy of a quilt, discovering all the components and parts that make up a quilt and finally learn the most common quilting types and techniques. Once you have learned all that, I will leave you with a series of handpicked quilting projects that you can use to unleash your creativity and become a quilting pro!

CHAPTER 1

What is Quilting?

In simplest terms, quilting is simply the art of stitching together three layers of cloth to form a decorative design. It can be done by hand or by machine. If you choose to do it by hand, it should be held in a quilting hoop or frame using special needles and a quilting thread. The challenge is to make the stitches straight and uniform. There are also people that hand stitch who are proud of their ability to make tiny stitches. On the other hand, machine stitching is done through a regular sewing machine. The challenge usually lies in learning how to smoothly feed the three layers of cloth to the sewing machine.

Each of the methods has advantages and disadvantages for their speed, design, and quality of work. Machine quilting is faster, more efficient, and more ideal for mass production. On the other hand, hand quilting gives the quilt a softer look, and it has more dimensions than machine quilting.

Patchwork and quilting are two distinct art forms, but they can be combined to create more beautiful products.

THE HISTORY OF QUILTING

To this day, scholars are unable to agree on the humble beginnings of quilting, precisely where and when it originated. In history, we find the first mention of a quilted garment during the Bronze Age, which, based on radiocarbon dating methods was made between 3218–3035 B.C.; this also coincides with the start of the First Dynasty of Ancient Egypt where we find evidence of the first quilted garment worn by an Egyptian Pharaoh. Following this train of thought, the sewing techniques used, such as piecing, appliqué, and quilting, must have been known, practiced, and perfected thousands of years before. The earliest reference to sewing and piecing can be found in Genesis 3:7 of the Holy Bible, which says, "They (Adam and Eve) sewed fig leaves together and made themselves aprons."

From then on, there have been several discoveries made by archaeologists such as the quilted rug in Mongolia dated approximately 100 BC to 200 AD, followed by numerous references made in literature and early civilization. Towards the end of the 11th century during the High and Late Middle Ages, Crusaders transported quilted items from regions between Western Asia and Egypt, now known as the Middle East.

During the European Middle Ages, 14th-century knights wore quilted gambesons under their armor to keep themselves warm, or over their armor to protect their metal armor from weather damage. These gambesons were made of linen or wool stuffed with horsehair or scrap cloth, designed with button openings upfront.

One of the valuable existing quilts presently housed at the Victoria and Albert Museum in London is a 14th-century Sicilian-designed European bed quilt made of wool-padded linen depicting scenic center blocks from the legend of Tristan.

Egyptian and Mediterranean trade routes were a perfect channel for the transport of quilting cloths and techniques, which became a valued addition to 5th-century European needlework. However, it was not until after the return of the Crusaders from the Middle East wherein quilted beddings, clothing, and other items made waves in Europe.

The subsequent influence of the medieval armored knights' quilted gambesons gave way to the quilted doublet, which became part of fashionable gentleman's wardrobe from the 14th to the 17th centuries. During the same time, the popularity of quilted clothing, doublets, and tunics spread across Europe, particularly in France, Germany, England, and Italy.

During the late 15th century, Christopher Columbus's discovery of America led to new trade routes, and eyes became focused not only on Europe but across the globe in Africa, Asia, and America. Amidst all these developments, the practice of quilting, embroidery, and needlework got caught amongst the rush of new fabrics techniques and fashion towards the New World.

American pioneering women made use of paper quilting, constructing paper patterns from every usable scrap of paper they could collect, such as letters, old newspapers, and catalogs. Each piece of fabric was carefully basted around the paper patterns and sandwiched between old quilts, these papers relayed untold stories and hardships of pioneer life. They also made summer quilts, which were made without backing, and worn in the same way as today's fashionable shawls.

During the 19th century, quilting techniques merged with embroidery, appliqué, and other sewing techniques as frugal women made quilts using blankets or worn-out quilts which had seen better days, sandwiched between whole new cloths instead of the pieced blocks which are in vogue today.

Quilting as a decorative art gained popularity in the 20th century, with eastern influences, particularly from India and China, whose textile art sense was more developed compared to the west.

Today's quilting techniques and patterns creativity are unbridled, with readily available materials, tools, and sewing technology. Moreover, with computer technology, one can choose from among several quilt design software such as Corel Draw, Adobe Illustrator, Windows Paintbrush, Mac Super Paint, Adobe Photoshop, and Aldus Freehand, to create unique designs to mix and match with available textile prints.

QUILTING FOR BEGINNERS

CHAPTER 2

Quilting Tools To Get Started

SEAM RIPPER

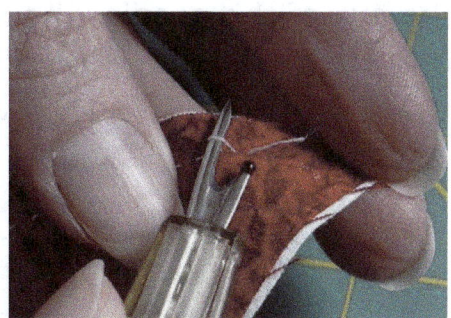

Sometimes stitches are not as smooth, straight, or small as we would like. Or you may have gotten a knot in your thread, or the thread broke, and you need to start over. A seam ripper can help you remove stitches quickly. Use a good light to work under, so you can see the stitches. Take your time, so you will not snag the fabric. If you pull a thread that is part of the fabric, you may ruin the piece and have to cut a new one. Ripping out goes more quickly if you cut every third stitch, and then pull the thread out.

THIMBLES

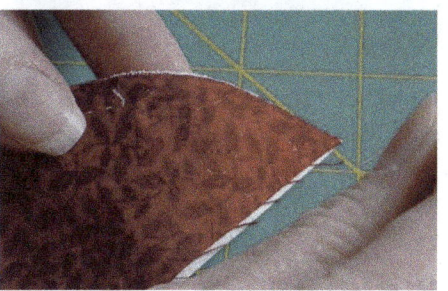

You will need a thimble or something to protect your fingers from the sharp point of the needle. It is an occupational hazard of hand-sewing, and experts need thimbles just as much as beginners. You will develop a callus on the finger that is below the fabric when you are quilting, but a thimble is your friend. Most of us have seen a traditional metal thimble, but there is a wide variety of materials and types of thimbles in the market. Some may fit your fingers better than others. Here are a few: a leather one with a metal disc in the tip, a metal one, and a band made of leather and plastic.

There are thimble pads made of leather with a sticky backing, so you can stick them on your finger to protect it from the needle's point. Place these pads wherever you need them. They are easier to wear than a regular thimble, which can get uncomfortable or hot.

If you have long fingernails, you may want a thimble with an open-top or a band thimble. As you sew, you may find that you push the eye of the needle with the side of the thimble, not with the end of it. Remember, there are no rules. Do whatever is comfortable for you.

PATTERNS OR TEMPLATES

You will need a template for each of the pieces in your quilt block. You use templates to cut the fabric pieces that go in the quilt block. The plastic sheets made for templates are: thin but sturdy, last longer than cardboard, and do not lose shape as the cardboard does. Template plastic has a grid printed on it to help you cut out the proper size of the pattern easily and quickly.

PENCILS OR FABRIC MARKERS

You may use mechanical pencils with fine lead, or other marking tools to mark seam lines and quilting lines on your fabric. Press lightly. The marks must wash out when you are finished quilting. That is why you do not use a ballpoint or felt-tip pen. Even marking pens that have water-soluble ink can cause problems if the heat of the iron sets the ink in the fabric.

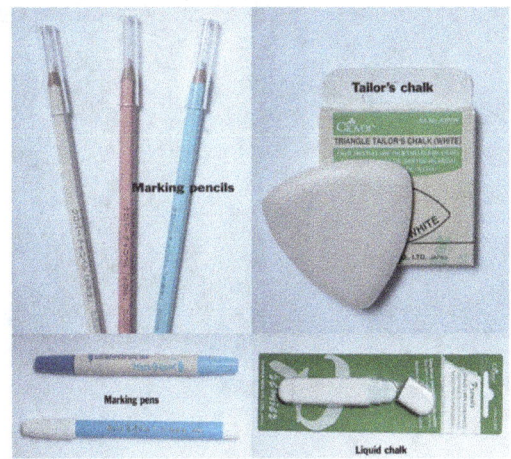

BRASS SAFETY PINS

Brass safety pins are used for holding the three layers of the quilt together. Brass is the best material because it does not catch rust, which comes in handy if the quilt project gets wet, or takes a long time to complete.

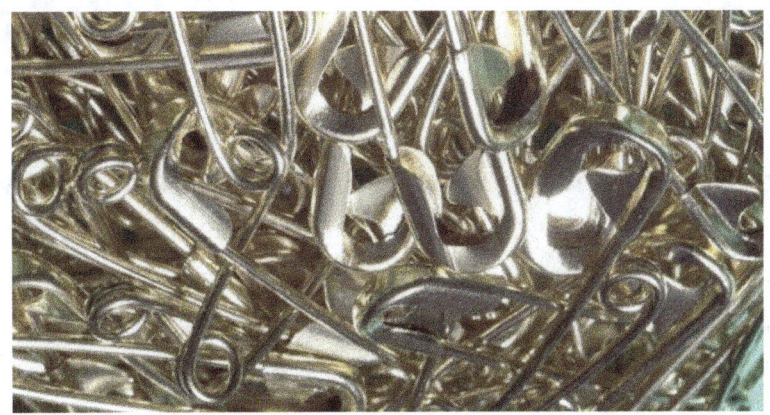

LONG QUILTING PINS, SILK PINS

There are different sizes of pins, just as there are different sizes of needles. Quilt pins are longer than regular pins, so they can hold all the layers of fabric together. These pins often have colored glass balls, or fabric tops so you can see them in the fabric, or if you drop them on the carpet. You will need pins to hold pieces of fabric together until you sew the seam. Remove the pins as you sew, and put them in a pin box, or a pin cushion.

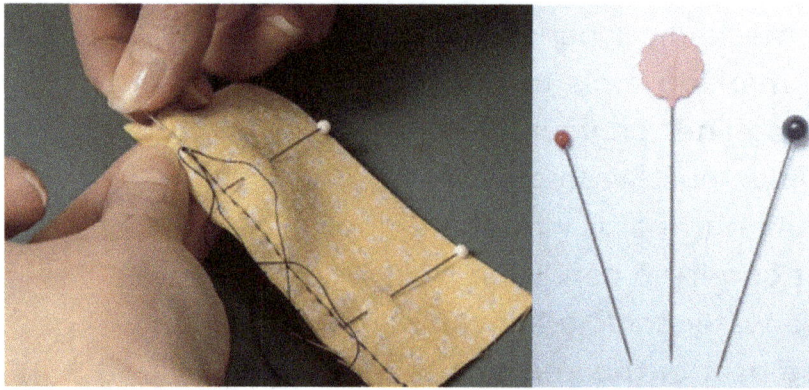

PIN CUSHION

It is important to keep your pins together safely, so you or your kids do not end up stepping on them. The one in the picture is magnetized, so the pins cannot fall out. In the common red 'Tomato' style pin cushion, the little strawberry on top is an emery bag. You can sharpen your needles and pins by sticking them into the bag several times.

IRON

You will need to use a steam iron for pressing the seams. This is very important for the appearance of the finished project, but you will also be pressing seams as you sew them. Use the permanent-press setting, so you do not scorch the fabric. Press the seam onto the darker fabric so that it does not show through the light fabric when you look at it from the front.

QUILTING FABRICS

The most important aspect of making a quilt is to choose the right fabric. Unfortunately, with the many styles, colors, patterns, types, and even textures, it is challenging to choose which fabric you should use for your quilting projects. While it is more of your personal preference, there are still rules when choosing the right fabric.

TYPES OF FABRICS FOR QUILTING

Cotton: Cotton is considered as the most popular fabrics used in making quilts today. 100% cotton fabric is strong and very easy to use. They are not as bright or rich in color as compared to cotton mixes like cotton/polyester. Although this may be the case, pure cotton fabric is very good at keeping shape and also timeless. They come in different kinds of patterns and colors. Moreover, most people prefer cotton because they do not have a sensitivity to it. This is the reason why quilted fabrics for children are made from 100% cotton.

Flannel: Flannel is another popular material used in making quilts. It is soft and very warm. Thus it is a great material for making baby items.

Silk: Silk is a luxurious and elegant fabric that you can use to make quilts. However, silk fabrics are very expensive, and they can also be slippery, thus making this type of fabric difficult to work with for beginners.

Velvet: Velvet is another type of luxury fabric, but it can also be used as a quilting fabric. Unlike silk, it has a rich and plush texture that can easily be worked with, even for beginners.

Corduroy: Corduroy is known for its interesting texture and sturdy built. It has a ribbed or textured pattern that will make your quilt look very intriguing. Corduroy has an informal look that adds quirkiness to your quilt.

Denim: Denim fabric is used in making blue jeans, and it provides informal quirk to quilting.

TIPS FOR CHOOSING THE RIGHT FABRICS

There are certain things that you need to know while choosing the right fabric for your quilting fabrics:

- Choose a colorfast fabric. Some fabrics bleed when you wash them, and this can ruin the whole design of your patchwork. When choosing a fabric, make sure that it is colorfast. However, if you are not sure if your fabric is colorfast, you can always wash it before using it.

- Choose a fabric with a tight weave. When you make a patchwork, you have the intention of using the finished product for a long time. Make sure that the fabric comes with a tight weave so that it can withstand years of washing and use. Choose a moderately dense, or woven fabric for your patchwork.

- Always start with 100% cotton fabric if you are a beginner. As an inexperienced quilter, you need to get used to working with the needles, and also your design. 100% cotton is very easy to work with, so you can never go wrong, unlike with silk and velvet, but if you do make mistakes, you can easily re-stitch your mistake.

- Cut the pieces the same way – all facing up. This is especially true if you are working with patterned fabric. This is to make sure that you do not waste your fabric by cutting it the wrong way.

- Always remember the color theory when selecting your fabric. Make sure that all your fabrics have the same balance and depth. Know about warm and cool colors and the effect of matching different colors on your fabric.

- Take into consideration the responses of people to the type of fabric and color that you use for your quilt, especially if you will give the quilt to someone as a gift. Customize the quilt and use the favorite color, fabric, or patterns of the recipient.

- Buy a backing material with the same weight and color of the top of the patchwork. This is to make the patchwork look impeccable.

- Buy a little more fabric than that which you will usually need for the project. This is to ensure that you will have enough fabric to work with, and also to prevent you from doing emergency fabric shopping in the middle of the day.

- Avoid synthetic or mixed fabrics because they are very difficult to deal with, especially if you are a beginner. These types of fabrics tend to pucker along the seams. Although they appear more vibrant in color than cotton, only experienced quilters can work with them. Other types of fabrics that should be avoided are: knitted, crepe, and stretch fabrics because they are very difficult to work with.

FABRIC MARKERS

Fabric markers allow you to mark fabrics with the patterns or designs that you want. Fabric markers can easily be washed off so that they do not destroy the appearance of the quilt. There are different types of fabric markers that you can use, depending on the composition of the fabric. The basic types of fabric markers that you can choose include pencils, chalk, and water-soluble markers.

QUILTING HOOPS AND FRAMES

Quilting hoops and frames are very important in making large patchworks, like bed-size comforters. They come in many shapes, styles, and sizes. Quilting hoops and frames have the same function, although they look different. A quilting hoop is made up of two round pieces with one slightly larger than the other where the fabric will be inserted. Quilting frames, as the name implies, are four-sided and self-supporting. It is used in making very large quilts.

CUTTERS

Cutting the quilting fabric is very important in making patchwork. Each piece should be precisely aligned to prevent an uneven appearance on the finished product. There are many cutters that you can use, but many experienced quilters use rotary cutters because they offer stability and precise slices at all times.

SHEARS OR SCISSORS

There is no doubt that you will need to have a pair of sharp fabric cutting scissors. This means that they are not your go-to scissors when you need to open up a bag of chicken tenders, or you need to pierce the frozen bag of veggies. These scissors will be specifically used for quilting.

Make sure that you can hold your scissors with a steady hand. If you go with the pair of shears, they will have a smaller hole for your fingers, but then a large hole for several fingers to fit in. Shears also have bent handles so that they can slide easily along a flat surface while you cut.

If you are not used to shears, they can be a bit tricky to get the hang of. I prefer scissors over shears because shears are difficult for me to handle. Scissors are typically used for small areas to trim down, and for cutting through excess fabric. Shears are used generally for large cutting jobs such as patchwork pieces.

You will also need a good pair of scissors reserved specifically for paper cutting. This is because when you follow two patterns for your template's quilts, you will be cutting templates out of plastic and or cardboard. For this reason, your scissors must be sharp. You will probably replace your paper cutting scissors more frequently, and a lot more often than you will replace your fabric cutting shears or scissors.

QUILTING MACHINES

Quilting machines are the equipment all quilters want to own. Quilting machines can range from simple sewing machines to specialized long-arm quilting machines. Quilting machines are necessary for quilters who are working on large and numerous projects.

CROCHET HOOK, BODKIN, TOOTHPICK OR COCKTAIL STICK

A crochet hook, bodkin, toothpick, or cocktail stick all serve similar purposes in quilting, which is to integrate the stuffing, or wadding into the design.

Aside from the above supplies, a quilting template would also be helpful, especially for beginners. Like sewing patterns, templates would help to produce a standard image that is pleasing to the eye, enable easy reproduction, and even be used as a teaching tool to impart newly acquired knowledge to others.

BATTING

Choosing the batting is an important part of the quilt-making process. The good thing is that, as long as you choose quality batting, there is no wrong answer.

Polyester batting has a nice drape, and it resists creasing. Cotton batting is also a great option. It has an amazing softness and is perfect for bed quilts. Ultimately, the best option is to try all different kinds of batting and see what you prefer.

NEEDLES

That is right, plain hand sewing needles. They can be purchased in packages of only one size or a variety of sizes. What you need will depend on what you plan on using to hold your quilt together. For many projects, however, regular hand sewing needles will do. For others, you might want a tapestry needle if you are planning on using yawn, or some other thick thread, for topstitching.

Needles come in sizes ranging from number 1 through 12. They are also categorized as being either sharks or between. Sharps are generally the all-purpose needle that is used for appliqué and piercing fabrics. Between are what you will need for quilting. The higher you get on the number range for needles, the finer and shorter your needle will be. For quilting, you will want a range between 7 and 12.

A universal needle can be used both for piecing and machine quilting. However, if you are using a specialty thread, or fabric other than cotton, you will probably want to use a different needle. Check the thread manufacturers' suggestions for more guidance.

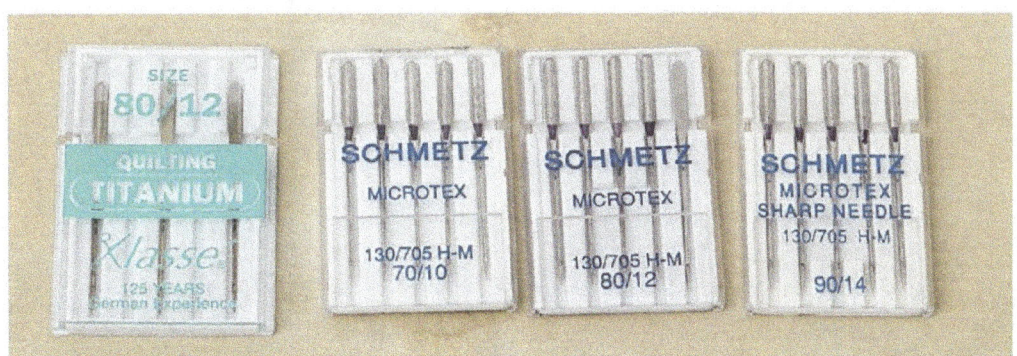

CHAPTER 3

Anatomy of a Quilt

PARTS OF A QUILT

BATTING

Batting refers to the single piece of fabric that will go on the underside of the quilt. You can use anything from an old sheet to a second quilt top, but many people prefer to use a solid color that coordinates with the colors on the top of the quilt. Between the two layers, you'll place a layer of batting. This is the insulation that gives the quilt its warmth. If you are planning on making a light summer quilt, batting is not necessary. For warm, winter quilts, you may want to use a very thick layer in the center to give it extra weight.

The two most significant factors in choosing batting are loft and fibers.

Loft describes the thickness of your batting. Low loft means thin, and high loft means thick. The low loft is better if you are planning to use a running stitch (by machine, or by hand) to attach your three layers later on. This will result in a thinner quilt. High-loft batting is best for comforter-like quilts that only need to be tied.

Fiber refers to what the batting is made of.

1. Polyester is the least expensive among the three fibers listed here. It is good to use if you plan on sewing by hand. However, it tends to 'beard', meaning

the fibers move through the fabric, and out the quilt if your stitches are not spaced closely enough.

2. Cotton is thicker than polyester, and a much better option if you are planning on using a sewing machine. It tends to shrink after the first wash and the quilt becomes softer. Whether this is a plus or minus, it depends on your preference.

3. The cotton blend is a mix of 80% cotton and 20% polyester. Price-wise, it is a little more expensive than polyester but less expensive than cotton. It also does not shrink as much and is also good for machine sewing.

In terms of size, your batting should be bigger than your front fabric (the one with the patchwork), and your backing should be bigger than your batting. It does not have to be a huge difference, a few inches is fine.

The reason for this is that during quilting, the batting and backing may shift from underneath your top layer. Having a few extra inches of space assures that the back of your quilt will not be shorter than the front.

TOP

This portion is the sewn and completed top layer.

BLOCK

A quilt block is the most basic part of the top layer of the quilt. Each quilt block is sewn in, and attached to another quilt block. The process goes on until the entire top layer is complete. But before the blocks can be created, several factors need to be considered first.

These include:

THE DESIGN

A lot of expert quilters recommend geometric designs for beginners. That is because making geometric shapes like squares and triangles with a piece of cloth is a lot easier. It is also quite easy to sew these shapes together to form a more interesting pattern.

Another quilt design that would be easy for beginners to accomplish is: piecing strips of cloth together. The strips can be obtained from various pieces of clothing that would otherwise be discarded.

THE SIZE OF THE QUILT

The size of a quilt mostly depends on what it will be used for. If it will be used as a bedding material, then you would have to know the dimensions of the bed itself. Bed sizes typically include king, queen, twin or double, and single beds. This means that the quilt bedding material would have to be large enough to cover the bed along with a little extra on the sides that can be tucked into the frame if needed.

Likewise, the size of a quilt table-topper would also depend on how large the actual table is. Quilts that will be used as placemats normally have to be at least 11 to 12 inches wide, and 15 to 18 inches long. Quilts that will be hung as wall decors can measure at least 9 inches square, or it can also be much larger than that. You can use the same principle when measuring the size of a quilt that would be used for: a crib, a baby's bed, as pillowcases, and so on.

BUILDING THE BLOCKS

After getting all the tools and learning more about the factors to consider, the next thing to do is to learn how to create a queen-size quilt.

Take note that in creating a quilt, you do not just pedal your way to your sewing machine, expecting it to create the quilt in just one sitting. Rather, you need to create it in sections. For beginners, I always recommend using a nine-square pattern composed of three rows of three squares, on top of each other. Hence, three in the bottom row, three in the middle, and then three on the top. It is ideal to lay this pattern before piecing it together, so you will see what you are doing.

When these squares have been pieced together, you can easily combine the squares to create your quilt. With a standard size of 3.5 inches by 3.5 inches for every fabric piece, the squares will be 10.5 inches. A basic queen-sized quilt is about eight squares by six squares.

You have the freedom to choose the fabric you want to use. You could either choose a conventional buck, a pattern or be creative. Remember, this is your quilt project, so you can do what you think feels right. Starters can simplify this by using a basic, dual-color pattern. But still, this completely depends on your preference.

The cheapest and easiest fabric to work in quilting is cotton. Many fabric stores will have enough supply of cotton fabric that is set for disposal which you can buy for a cheaper price or even ask for free.

If you are still learning how to quilt, it is practical to obtain some of this before investing in a premium roll of fabric. Oftentimes, you will stumble upon a big bundle of fabric that is ideal for practicing. You can even find a pattern, which you have never tried working with before.

For a proper quilt, you will need 48 blocks, each of nine inches, so you need to prepare 432 squares of fabric. This may seem overwhelming, but when you group them into various colors, it will be simpler to work with. For instance, it is easy to get up to 70 squares, from a yard of fabric. Hence, about five yards of fabric are enough to make a proper queen size quilt, with plenty of left-over squares in case you make some errors.

When you have prepared your squares, the next step is to choose the stuffing material. There are different options available, and practically, there is no recommended material. Various materials will provide your quilt with various textures, so you might want to take some time and try materials that you want the most.

A commonly used material for stuffing is still cotton, because of its texture, and since it is easy to work with. Cotton has higher breathability compared to other fabrics, and you can easily lay it flat. It is also very soft and wears well.

Another fabric that you can use is polyester. Although less expensive than cotton, there are some downsides in using this fabric. It could bunch in the quilt, particularly after several washings, and could even peek out through the cloth. This is not ideal if you have a dark, or colorful quilt, as the appearance can be ratty. But when it comes to providing warmth, polyester is a good fabric choice over cotton for the middle section.

Wool can also be used for stuffing. This fabric is the heaviest and the warmest material, so it is ideal if you are making a queen size quilt for winter. However, it could be a real trouble when it comes to cleaning as it gets heavier once wet, and it could also shrink. As such, dry cleaning is ideal. Moreover, wool could be more troublesome to work with, as it takes some effort to flatten and bend.

Then, you also need to find material for the bottom section, or the back sheet. You can choose a large piece of textile, or you can just buy a pre-sewn sheet at a textile store. The color depends on your choice, even though white is the top choice for a quilt.

SASHING

Sashing is the strips of fabric between quilt blocks.

QUILTING

It refers to the stitching that holds the three layers (quilt top, batting, and backing) together.

BINDING

The binding is the edge of the quilt, and it hides the unfinished edges of the top and the batting in the center. Binding can be made of anything, but most people use fabric or fabric tape that is cut on a bias. This helps give it the strength and lack of stretch necessary to hold everything together. You can find bias tape readymade at most craft or fabric shops, or you can cut your own from fabric you have in the house.

CORNERSTONES

These are also called sashing squares which connect sashing strips where they meet at block corners.

BACKING

The quilt backing serves as the binding of the entire quilt. Although it is not usually seen like the quilt top, it plays a very important role in keeping things together. It also shows how well or neat the quilt was made.

Attaching the back quilt is the hardest part, so take your time with this one. The first thing to do is to ensure that you have a flat, clean surface where you can work efficiently. Then make certain that your hands and feet are clean. You need to walk on your quilt, so you do not want to make the quilt dirty. You need to lay out your top quilt and place the stuffing material. Finally, complete it with your back quilt and start pinning.

You cannot use enough pins for this work. You need to create three layers, and these layers will munch up a lot, once you start sewing. Three layers is an ideal number to start, but you can always add more layers. Be sure to smooth the stuffing material as you go, and to continuously check for damage, or wrinkles as you work. Remember, it is a lot easier to re-pin than to re-sew.

More often than not, a part of the quilt will bunch up, which could happen when you are moving across the fabric. Hence, you need to be more innovative in working with your quilt. You need to use a heavy object to weigh down the sheets and lay them out. Just be sure to use a lot of pins.

Once you are done with the pinning, you need to check the needles and the thread. You can use cotton thread that matches the bottom sheet's color for the understitch, and a clear nylon thread for the topstitch.

I highly recommend that you run several test stitches in some spare fabric before you start to ensure that your sewing machine is properly calibrated and that the stitch patterns are well-aligned. Remember, it is better to find out that you have a bad needle on a test fabric than your actual quilt.

Because you are working with three layers of textiles, it is ideal to employ a walking foot. This will simplify your job and could help in minimizing the bunching. Begin on the outside long edge, and then work on for the long edges, rolling the quilt as you do so. When you are halfway, get the quilt and turn it around and begin from the other side. Be sure to keep rolling as you work, and do not rush. Be patient and take note, there is no need to go straight from one side to another as you are selecting your rows. If you are done with the length, it is time to work with the width. This is a bit easier since you have a shorter area to work on. Once done properly, the final seam can be smooth, thin, line across the blocks and your quilt body is complete.

QUILT SANDWICH

If you are working with a large project, you need to work in an area with a lot of space. Lay down the quilt sandwich on the floor. Make sure that the floor is clean so that dirt will not stick to the quilt sandwich.

Lay down the backing then smoothen it out using the palms of your hands. Lay the batting on top of the backing and make sure you leave even amounts of the batting material around the edges. Add the quilt top and make sure to get it in the center. Trim the backing or batting if you think they are large enough.

Once you have already laid down the quilt sandwich, you can now pin them. Find the center of the quilt and put a safety pin on it to hold the three layers together. This will prevent the quilt sandwich from sliding off. From the edges of the sash, measure 6 inches and pin the three layers. Do this until you have pinned the borders of the quilt sandwich. Smooth out the bubbles and creases along the way.

CHAPTER 4
The Different Types of Quilts

We all come to quilting because some technique or style has captured our hearts. There are dozens of techniques and each has its own following.

WHOLE CLOTH

Designing a full-size quilt as a single composition allows you to control the balance across the entire quilt. But the embellishing becomes more challenging as you deal with such a large undertaking.

However, some techniques can help reduce this difficulty factor.

No-Patchwork: Traditionally, "whole cloth quilts" are solid pieces of fabric that are quilted with a design. There is no piecing involved. These are also often referred to as "whitework quilts" because they gained popularity as stamped designs on white cloth. This is a great option when working with very dark fabric.

SCRAP QUILTS

It can be argued that any quilt made out of scrap fabric could be rightfully called a scrap quilt, but I'm using this term to specifically describe those quilts made out of squares or "scraps" of fabric that have no pattern or design to them. A true scrap quilt will be made up of multiple squares placed randomly through the quilt. The quilt may be tied rather than quilted, meaning that instead of quilting stitches joining the three layers together, pieces of yarn or ribbon are used to tie the layers together at regular intervals. Scrap quilts are arguably the easiest type to make and are often made by beginners as well as children who want to learn to sew and make their own quilts.

Scrap quilts can be very beautiful in their own way, with several different variations available. One variation is known as the Postage Stamp and is made up of very small pieces of fabric, most around 2-inches in size. When seen from across the room, the finished quilt is a riot of color and pattern and can be great for brightening up any room of your house.

PATCHWORK OR PIECED QUILT

One of the most popular quilt types is a patchwork or pieced quilt. As the name suggests, several patches of cloth are pieced and sewed together to form a pattern, and this process is called patchwork. Typically, each quilt is divided into symmetric sections, which are commonly referred to as blocks. Each of these blocks houses a patchwork sequence or pattern in it. Typically, each of these blocks has a similar pattern for symmetry in design. However, if you like, you may vary the design of the patchwork pattern by putting in different elements in each of the blocks. You may change the style, shape, and arrangement of patches in each of these blocks as per your liking.

Patchwork is both a skill and an art. Therefore, no matter how experienced a quilter you may be, you may make mistakes. While planning to make a patchwork quilt, there are a few things you must keep in mind. First, you must choose the pattern and colors carefully. It is always a good idea to get a second opinion on a pattern or color before finalizing it. This is particularly the case if you are making the quilt for someone else.

Second, the secret to good patchwork is consistency and matching patterns. Although having heterogeneity in patterns may seem like an interesting idea, the end product may not turn out to be as appealing as you desire.

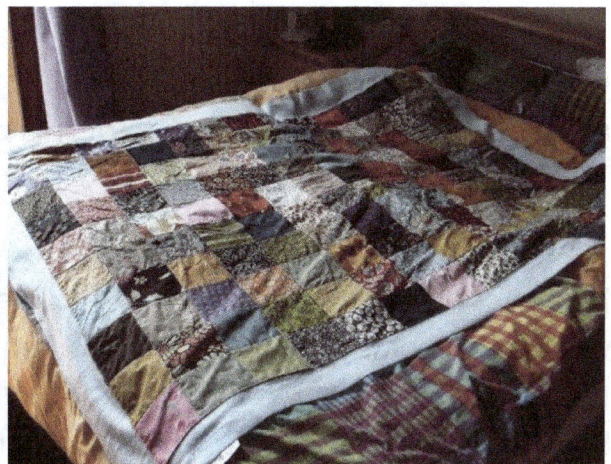

APPLIQUÉ QUILT

Appliqué is the method of placing fabrics with defined shapes on the background. The shaped fabrics are often sewn by hands or using a machine. This style of quilting provides a lot of freedom, and it also provides an interesting story to the entire quilt.

This piecing method uses scraps and is the best method for creating a block with fabrics of different weights and types. Prepare fabrics first by stabilizing them with a thin (knit is best) type of fusible or stitch-in interfacing if they are at all fancy. Especially do this for slippery fabrics such as satin, any dance or costume fabrics that stretch, loosely woven fabrics, or sheer fabrics. The result should be a patch that is flat and nicely behaves when it is joined with other fabrics.

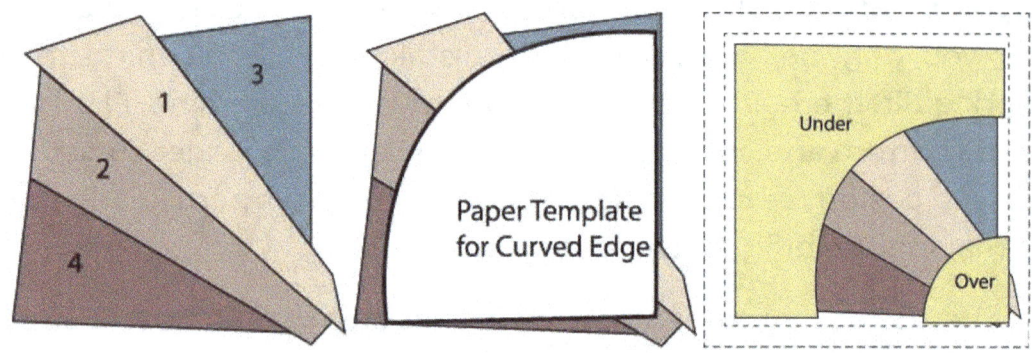

ART QUILTS AND WALL HANGINGS

The art quilt is simply art with the fabric serving, like the canvas, and the mediums are the fabric and thread. It is similar to a painting, but the images are sewn by hand. The purpose of this particular method is to turn fabric into a piece of art; thus, it is not made to keep you warm.

There is something that goes beyond quilting with an art quilt. The "artist" brings something so unique to a project there are no two alike. The art quilt will most decidedly not be used to keep bodies warm, but oh, the stories they tell… the messages they convey. You will not find pieced blocks in an art quilt, but will find unusual shapes and designs instead.

Once in a while, you may decide you want to learn a new technique but don't want to engage in an overly large project. If so, wall hangings and banners might be just the answer! Keep in mind that although for the most part quilting projects for our early settlers had a focus on maximizing the use of limited fabrics and making items to keep their families warm, that creative edge that lies within a quilter cries out for something more! Something decorative. Quilting has always been an art form, and as smaller children were taught the skills, smaller projects were designed to fill that need. During the process of learning quilting skills, many young women also learned a form of personal expression.

Quilts have not only been used as bed coverings, and even though wall hangings may have been made to also keep out cold air, as a creative décor item, women made wall quilts more elaborate than quilts made for every day. If you search for wall quilts today, because many of them do not require extensive cleaning and care, it is much easier to add more glitz and glam than quilting for durability.

Quilts in the Wall Hangings category use both modern and traditional quilting techniques, often mixed with other art concepts to create "art objects" from the fabric. Quilt artists more often base their project on personal experiences, imagery, and creative ideas than they use traditional patterns.

AMISH QUILTS

Like our ancestors, the Amish made quilts as a frugal way to use up fabric scraps; it also, over time transformed into a creative, artistic expression.

While the modern world stepped forward with every evolution experienced in quilting, the Amish tried to remove themselves from those temptations. Although very few Amish made quilts were known before the 1870s, they did gradually embrace the merits of quilting and over the next decade or so, quilting was quite common in their communities.

As most of us worked hard to use what was popular at any given time, the Amish long remained highly conservative and their quilts are easily identified as solid colors (brown, rust, black, blue). Although they kept the fabric plain, it was the quilting that made their work so popular. Intricate, decorative… swirling feathers, curves, and grids held their quilt sandwiches together.

Slowly, gradually… more colors were added to the mix: olive green, pumpkin, and an occasional dark red. Borders and center accents also became more accepted. While the rest of the country was lavishly embellishing crazy quilts, the Amish had stepped up to a few nine-patch patterns.

BLOCK QUILT

This style of quilting is very traditional. To make the design, a piece of patterned square fabric is used to create the overall design of the quilt. There are different designs available for this design, which include the nine-patch, churn dash, shoo fly, and prairie queen. Below is a list of the different techniques in block quilting.

- Nine-Patch: **The nine-patch is created by sewing five dark pieces of patches to four light squares in alternating order to create one block.**

- Shoo fly: **The shoo fly is a variation of the nine-patch style. This pattern is created by dividing the four corner pieces into dark and light triangles.**

- Churn dash: **This is another variation of the nine-patch design, and it combines the rectangle and triangles to create an expanded nine-patch style.**

- Prairie queen: **The prairie queen combines two big triangles in the corner while the middle section is made up of smaller four squares. The centerpiece is made up of one full-size square.**

MODERN QUILTS

Modern quilting is inspired by modern designs. Modern quilting can be done in different styles and in different ways. Blood colors, prints, and high contrasts are used in modern quilting. Graphic designs including solid colors, improvisational piecing, expansive negative space, minimalism, and alternate grid work are also some of its aspects.

New and enhanced designs and patterns have been used to give advanced looks to quilts. Excess time can be utilized in creating something beautiful, so it is a good activity to do in your leisure time. Most modern quilts are made from 100% cotton fabric. The two or three layers in the middle of the quilt are usually cotton, polyester, muslin, silk, or wool. Sometimes for sentimental reasons fabric from old clothes or old, tattered quilts are used in new quilts.

CHAPTER 5

Quilting Techniques

There are numerous types of quilting styles that you can do. Each of the styles differs in its history as well as the types of materials used. This section will discuss the different quilting styles that you can use to do your projects.

PAPER PIERCING

Also known as Foundation Piecing, Paper Piercing is a technique wherein the fabric is stitched on a paper foundation. The paper patterns come with lines and numbers as guides to create the quilt. With this type of quilting, quilters can create fantastic and precise designs even if they are beginners.

TYING

Tying is the simplest way to hold your quilt sandwich together, and it's often the first technique most people learn. You can use anything to tie your quilt, but most people prefer yarn as it holds securely and can come in so many different colors.

STITCH-AND-FLIP FOUNDATION PIECING

Most contemporary quilters stitch fabric patches to a foundation cloth using a method called stitch-and-flip foundation piecing. It is a very simple method that has some advantages.

- It is quick.

- It is a free-form type of piecing, so there is no marking or using templates.

- Because you are using a fabric foundation instead of paper, you do not have a paper to tear away.

- The seams do not distort. Often in the process of making blocks, you will use fabrics that are cut on the bias and this can distort a seam line. With fabric foundation piecing, you don't have this problem.

- The foundation fabric adds strength, so beading and embellishing is not a problem.

This method produces a different block every time you do it. It is difficult to reproduce exactly what you have done before.

FOUNDATION FABRIC

Your foundation cloth should be a lightweight cotton muslin, or if you recycle, you can use fabric from worn bedsheets and pillowcases. Most of my quilts have a foundation of old recycled fabrics. Cotton is preferable because you need to be able to iron it. Steer clear of using shiny, slippery synthetic fabric, because the purpose of a foundation cloth is to provide a stable base.

When choosing a foundation fabric, make sure it is thin but not so thin that it will tear easily. You will be hand embroidering through the top patch of fabric and the foundation cloth. If the combination of fabrics is too thick, you will tire or get frustrated at pulling your embroidery thread through. Apart from the fact that it is hard to create pleasing embroidery on thick, bulky seams, if the hand embroidery is no fun, you will soon become frustrated and tired of the project.

Notes:

Choose a block size you are comfortable with. I find any block between 6˝ (15.2 cm) and 12˝ (30.5 cm) is comfortable and does not take too long to complete.

Make sure your fabric has been washed and will not shrink.

Cut your foundation fabric square on grain (not bias) and add a seam allowance of at least ½″ (1.3 cm) all around the block. For example, for an 8″ (20.3 cm) square block, you will need a 9″ × 9″ (22.9 cm × 22.9 cm) piece of fabric.

Tip:

Why such a large seam allowance? Your block may start flat and square, but when you hand embroider it and add beads, and so on, it can pucker slightly and, in some cases, pull slightly out of shape. If you have a large seam allowance, you will be able to trim the block square before assembling the quilt. Leave yourself some wiggle room.

PIECING METHOD

There is no hard-and-fast rule about this, but the stitch-and-flip method works best if you start with a fabric patch that has an uneven number of sides. A piece with five or seven sides is ideal. If you are a beginner, work with five sides until the process feels natural to you.

Tips

- Generally, I try and use similar-weight fabrics on a project, as this saves headaches when it comes to assembling. I try to avoid the situation where I have to piece together a thick block to a thin block. For instance, when a block with thick velvet down one side needs to be stitched to a block with thin, shiny satin, it can lead to frustration. To avoid this, I keep the weight and thickness of all the fabrics about the same.

- Sometimes, however, there is a fantastic bit of velvet or tapestry I simply want to use. It sings to me! In this situation, I start the block with the special but problematic fabric. The other pieces will be added around it, preventing it from ending up on an outer seam.

- Use a good quality machine thread. I don't spend time obsessively matching thread to the color of each patch added to the block. Instead, I think about tone. For light fabrics, I use white or cream thread. On darker fabrics, I use black or gray thread.

- It doesn't matter if you work in a clockwise or counterclockwise direction, as long as you don't change direction during the piecing.

APPLIQUÉ

Appliqué is a sewing technique that is not confined to quilting. Many people who sew have done some type of appliqué before, whether decorating clothing or creating a piece of fabric art. Creating an appliqué for a quilt is the same. The differences lay in what you'll be doing as your overall design.

Some people choose to make an appliqué quilt by taking a single image and placing it onto the center of a quilt block, stitching the various blocks together to form a quilt top. Other people will take a single large piece of cloth and appliqué multiple images onto the cloth to form a larger design. Both are viable ways of creating an appliqué-style quilt. If you've never done appliqué before, you may want to start with a sampler, creating some pieced and some appliqué blocks to learn both techniques at once. Or you may want to start with creating a single appliqué image and repeating it again and again over the blocks of a quilt to perfect your stitches. If you are familiar with the appliqué technique, you can try mapping out a larger design onto a small quilt – a wall hanging or a crib quilt – to get the hang of designing and stitching over a large surface before moving on to backing, binding, and quilting the layers.

There are a lot of different stitches that can be used to appliqué from blanket stitches to whip stitches. The backstitch is probably the easiest to master on a quilt, however, because you can tie in the stitches to the finished quilting. To create an appliqué quilt using blocks and to get used to the stitching, you can try this technique.

STITCHING IN THE DITCH

When you first begin to hand quilt and stitch your three layers together for the first time, it will take you a little while to get used to the rocking stitches and to keep the length and size of your stitches even. Therefore, you need a way to practice that doesn't require you to also follow a pattern of stitches, and that can help disguise the uneven nature of your work until it improves. One of the best ways to do this is to stitch in the ditch.

Stitching in the ditch means that you'll follow the outline of each one of your quilt pieces, putting your quilting stitches in the "ditch" that the seams make between two pieces. When complete, the stitches give your quilt the dimension and depth it needs and holds everything together well, but you won't see the stitches unless you go looking for them. This is a great method of hiding your beginner's mistakes. Don't worry, by the time you've quilted an entire top your stitches will become good enough to begin putting them out in the open where they can be seen.

HAND QUILTING

As the name implies, hand quilting is all about using: a quilting hoop, or frame, a needle, and thread to create the quilt. When doing hand quilting, begin in the middle of the quilt by attaching the hoop or frame to it. If you are doing an appliqué quilt, sew around the edges of the shapes to give them a puffed-up look. Use small stitches, and do not rush with your sewing. If you are making a patchwork, start in the middle and follow the lines of the squares. Use the loop or frame to secure the area where you are sewing. If you do cross-hatching, draw lines on the quilt top so that you can have an even look on the quilt.

MACHINE QUILTING

Machine quilting uses a machine. Thus it is easier for you to finish a quilting project. Cross hatching is easily achieved in machine quilting as the machine comes with markers so that you can easily measure the distance of the lines that you want to make.

CHAPTER 6

Basic Care and Laundering

SHOULD YOU PRE-WASH YOUR FABRIC?

- Whether or not you should pre-wash your fabric is a matter of choice. Some people do not like to pre-wash the fabric because crisp, brand new fabric off the bolt is easier to cut with precision. Not pre-washing is only recommended if you are using the highest quality, 100% cotton fabric that is made for quilting. These have fewer problems than lower-end fabrics have, like the colors bleeding together during a wash. If you are using fabric that is older or lower in quality, you should pre-wash it before you cut it. That will take care of possible problems with shrinkage and color bleeding.

- One piece of advice that you should follow is to be consistent with your decision. Either pre-wash all the material that you will use in the quilt, or not pre-wash any of it. If you purchased fabric but will not be using it for a while, do not pre-wash until you are ready to start your quilt.

How to Prewash - Separate your fabric colors into darks and lights. Set your washing machine to a gentle cycle using cool water. Use a mild soap made for quilts. After the wash, shake out the material gently and put it in the dryer. Set the drying to low heat. As soon as the fabric is dry, remove it from the dryer. Or, you can take it out when it is still a little bit damp. Then press.

PROS TO PREWASHING:

- It will preshrink the material up to five percent so that when you wash the finished quilt, it will not shrink so much.

- It will wash out any extra dye from the darker colored materials so that when you wash your quilt, color bleeding will be minimized. Some fabrics will continue to bleed in the following wash after the pre-wash. So, if you are concerned about that, use a product like Retayne before your first wash to keep the dyes from running.

- It will wash away chemical residuals that may cause skin irritation for some people.

- You should always pre-wash flannel if you will use it with cotton. Flannel shrinks a lot, sometimes up to two times the shrinkage of regular cotton. To be on the safe side, test your fabric for shrinkage by cutting out a square test piece and measure its size, then wash it, and measure it again. If the shrinkage is significantly more than cotton, and you only pre-washed your cotton fabric once, you should pre-wash the flannel two times That way, when you wash your finished quilt, the rate of shrinkage of the flannel and cotton will be about the same.

CONS TO PRE WASHING:

- Pre-cut strips and small pieces will twist together and may get stuck in the washing machine's agitator.

- Some people just like the look of a quilt that shrinks after a wash, with all the puckering and bumps.

- Without pre-washing, the fabric maintains the vibrancy and richness of the original colors.

- Without pre-washing, the crispness of the new fabric right off of the bolt makes it easier to make precise cuts.

- If the quilt will only be used for decorative purposes, the fabric does not need to wash.

You can do a quick colorfast test before you cut your fabric. This is important if you will use a light fabric with a dark fabric. Fill your sink with cool water with a little bit of soap in it. Then, take a small sample piece of material and soak it for around 30 minutes. If you see color in the water, then it bleeds. You will need to use Retayne to prevent bleeding or not use this fabric at all. If you do decide to use it, remember to pre-wash all of the other materials that you plan to use for your quilt.

If you do not see color in the water, do one more test. Put the material on a piece of white paper towel until the material has dried. If the paper towel still has no color, then your material is ready to be used.

PERFORMING A BLEEDING TEST

A bleeding test is most of the time carried out to assure the stability of dyes. There are many incidents that the quilting cotton loses its dyes in less of the time when washed. The loosing on dye is also referred to as bleeding in quilting terminology. The chances of losing dyes are more in red and purple color.

The dyes will not only fade out but will also stain the other fabrics. Also, it will make unwanted, faded patches on the quilt pattern that took a long time to make.

Follow these steps to perform the test to make sure your fabric is not bleeding:

- First, submerge the fabric in water. The water is already made soapy before submerging takes place. The water temperature is kept normal for the test.

- The fabric needs to be adjusted for about half a minute in the soapy water. Then the next thing to look at is watercolor. If the water becomes discolored, then it means that the fabric is bleeding and can also affect other fabrics.

- Even if the water looks clear, you can try one thing to prevent damage to other fabric. Without rinsing, consider taking out the patch and place it on the top of a white towel. If the color blotches to the white towel, there are good chances that the dyes will transfer to patches that are adjacent at the time of washing the quilt.

- Lastly, take out all the soap and dry patches. If, even after doing the steps above the bleeding continues, then do not consider using the fabric again.

PREVENTING THE FABRIC FROM FRAYING

- The common problem many beginners face while pre-washing the fabric is that the strings become too loose at the time of washing.

- When the fabrics tangle in the wash with each other, they twist, and all the grains pull at the point of the fabric. And to make fabric wrinkle-free, care must be taken to remove all the threads that are tangled up, before putting it into the dryer.

- The technique to remove all the strings is extremely easy. From each corner, you need to cut off the tiny triangular part before washing them. For the tryout, you can start with ½ inch or less than that just to see the effectiveness of the technique. The little fraying will still be there but do not worry as it is not sufficient to create a bunch of knots.

- Even the little of the snip can make a huge difference, so it is advisable to try this technique the following time you consider prewashing.

CHAPTER 7

Step By Step Quilt Projects

GARDEN PILLOW

Bring the garden indoors with this lovely patchwork and appliqué pillow. One Busy Bee block combined with some blanket stitch appliqué units makes this a great project for a beginner.

You will need...

- Tan fabric for background 7¾ in (20 cm) (width of fabric)

- Cream-on-cream fabric for background 7 in (17.8 cm) square

- Tan check for background 6½ in (16.5 cm) square

- Three assorted blueprints 6 in (15.2 cm) square of each

- Three assorted red prints 6 in (15.2 cm) square of each

- Three assorted burgundy prints 6 in (15.2 cm) square of each
- Blue floral print for pillow back 20 in (50.8 cm) square
- DMC stranded embroidery cotton (floss): red (816), soft blue (932), and burgundy (3802)
- Calico 20 in (50.8 cm) square
- Wadding (batting) 20 in (50.8 cm) square
- Blue floral fabric for binding 3 in (7.6 cm) (width of fabric)
- Zip 15¾ in (40 cm) long
- Pillow pad 18 in (46 cm) square

Finished size: 18 in (46 cm) square

Step 01

CUTTING THE FABRICS

From the tan background fabric cut one piece 6½ in × 18½ in (16.5 cm × 47 cm), four pieces 3½ in × 6½ in (8.9 cm × 16.5 cm), and one 6½ in (16.5 cm) square.

From the tan check background fabric cut one 6½ in (16.5 cm) square.

From the cream fabric, cut four 3½ in (8.9 cm) squares.

From assorted print fabrics, cut a total of nine 2½ in (6.4 cm) squares.

Step 02

MAKING THE BUSY BEE BLOCK

Assemble the nine-patch block from the nine 2 1/2 in (8.9 cm) squares. With random color placement and using 1/4 in (6 mm) seams, join the squares to form three rows of three. Join the three rows together to form the nine-patch.

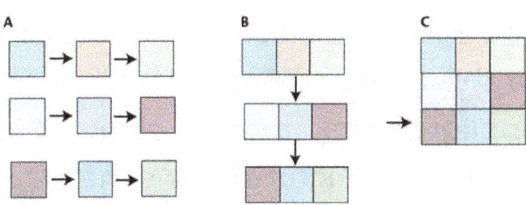

Step 03

Take two of the 3 1/2 in × 6 1/2 in (8.9 cm × 16.5 cm) pieces and join them to the top and bottom of the nine-patch unit. Now join a 3 1/2 in (8.9 cm) cream square to each end of a 3 1/2 in × 6 1/2 in (8.9 cm × 16.5 cm) rectangle and join this unit to one side of the nine-patch block. Repeat for the other side to make the arrangement shown.

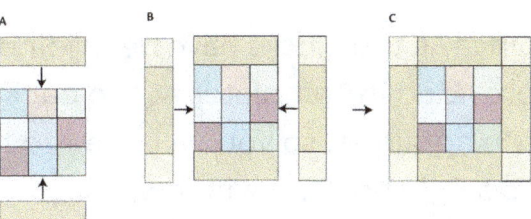

Step 04

MAKING THE BACKGROUND BLOCKS

The Busy Bee block now needs to be joined to the fabric pieces that will make up the appliqué backgrounds, using ¼ in (6 mm) seams. The picture shows the arrangement of the pieces.

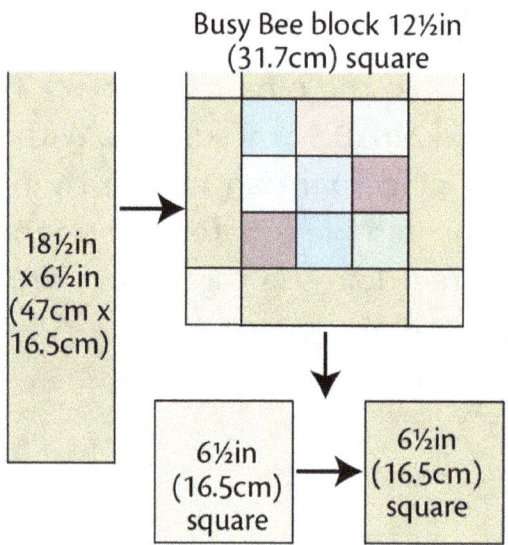

Step 05

WORKING THE APPLIQUÉ

Once all the blocks have been joined, you can work the appliqué. Use the shapes provided in Templates at the back of the book. The fusible web was used to do the appliqué, so you will need to reverse the shapes using a light source such as a lightbox or a window.

Step 06

When the appliqués are fused into position using two strands of embroidery thread to work, blanket stitch around the edges of the shapes, matching the red, soft blue, and burgundy thread colors to the fabrics.

Step 07

QUILTING

I hand quilted my pillow front, layering the front with wadding (batting) and calico and quilting around each appliqué shape. A simple crisscross pattern was quilted in the nine-patch block.

Step 08

INSERTING THE ZIP AND MAKING UP

From the pillow backing fabric cut two pieces 18 1/2 in × 9 3/4 in (47 cm × 24.8 cm). Press 1/2 in (1.3 cm) to the wrong side of the fabric along one long side of each piece.

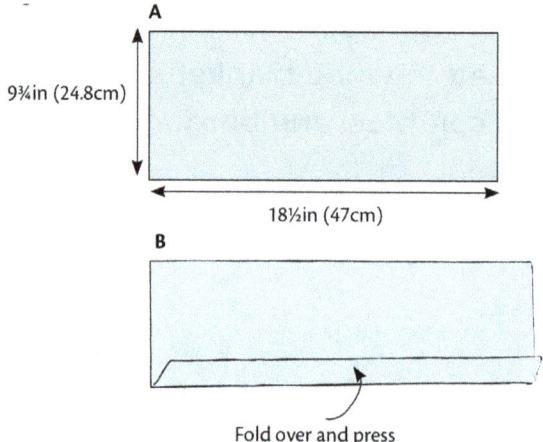

Step 09

Place the zip in position on one side and pin in place. Using the zip foot on your machine, stitch the first side of the zip into place (Fig 5). Position and pin the other side of the zip and stitch in place.

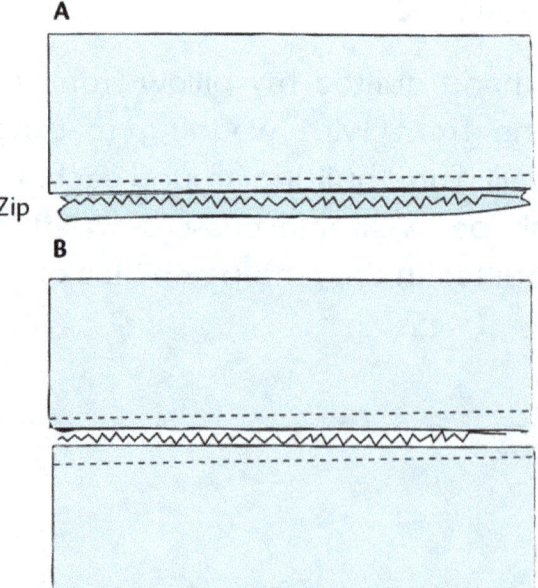

Step 10

Take the back and the front of the pillow, place them wrong sides together (right sides out) on a flat surface and pin them together. Sew the pieces together all around the edge, using a 1/4 in (6 mm) seam.

Step 11

BINDING

To bind the pillow, cut a strip 1 1/2 in (3.8 cm) wide × the necessary length (about 80 in/203 cm), cut on the straight grain. Press in 1/4 in (6 mm) down the length of the strip. Press the binding and then insert the pillow pad inside the cover to finish.

SIMPLE BABY BLUSH

Sometimes, the best way to start a quilt is to go with something small, something for a baby! I love making baby quilts. They can double as a small mat (if you use a thicker batting like I tend to prefer with baby blankets) for children not yet mobile to lay on inside and outdoors. A good baby blanket/quilt size is about 46" x 46".

MATERIALS

- 8 Different fat quarters of printed fabric (or 48 different 5.5" squares)
- Yards of 54" wide (thick) SOLID fabric for the sashing and backing.

Step 01

Each fat quarter will get you 6 - 5.5" squares. When you are done cutting, you will have 48 different squares. Out of the solid fabric, cut your backing first, a 50" or 54" square. If you are worried about messing up somehow, and having extra fabric will make you feel comfortable, then, by all means, go with the bigger square of 54". However, 50" is what you'll likely trim the backing down to, but it's nice to know the extra 4" is there to keep you from panicking.

Step 02

Now that you have your squares and backing, you'll need to cut 3" strips out of the solid fabric for sashing. The sashing is trimmed as you go, so just keep the pieces together.

Step 03

The key to the success of this quilt is the placement of the squares. You will start with:

- Squares in the middle. Sew them to the right so that they become a square of 4 squares. Make the other strips required in the quilt:

- In between the first four squares and the second, a larger square (or line of blocks) will be sashing. To the right of the first square will be a strip of five blocks long. The middle will be 3 blocks long, and then the left will be 5 blocks long, with the bottom at another 3 blocks long.

- The final block of squares, starting from the right side, will have 6 blocks on the strip. The top will have 8 blocks an, the left will have 6. The bottom will have another 8 blocks.

- Sew the blocks together first to create these strips. Press the seam in the same direction, and then start with the original centerpiece of four squares. For each part of the sashing, you will see a strip along the side of the center block, trimming the sashing ends to be even with the center block. Please remember always to cut the sashing ends to be even with the center block.

QUILTING FOR BEGINNERS

MODERN GRANNY MINI QUILT/PILLOW

Level: confident beginner

Seam allowance ¼ in

Finished project size approximately 21 in X 21 in

Finished project: mini quilt or pillow

MATERIALS

- Scraps of 8 fabrics (each scrap should be about 7 in X 13 in To ensure plenty of room to cut rectangles
- 3/8 yd White fabric
- 5/8 yd fabric backing for a pillow or 2/3 yd backing for a quilt
- 1/4 yd fabric for binding

CUTTING INSTRUCTIONS

WOF = Width of Fabric

- Three 2 in X 4 in Rectangles in 8 different fabrics
- Four 3.5 in White squares
- Two 12 in White squares (see cutting below) *
- One 21 in Square for the back (any fabric)—if you intend to machine quilt, add an inch or two to every side.
- Three 2.5 in x WOF for the binding (any fabric)

* Once you have cut out the two 12 in white squares, you need to cut the square on the diagonal so that you have 4 equal triangles.

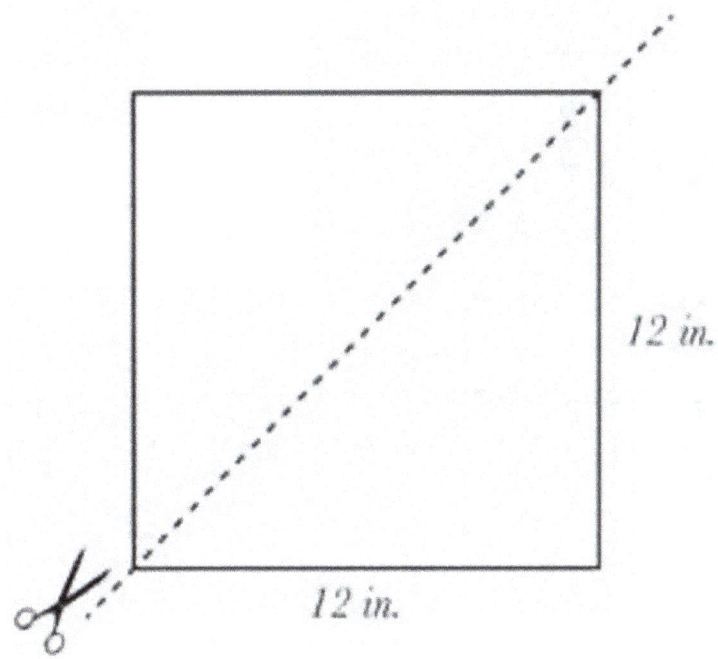

Step 01

BLOCK ASSEMBLY

Sew together four 2 in 4 in rectangles together. Press then cut in half. Repeat until you have twelve sets of strips like this. Then layout 8 of these in a row and sew together for the middle part of the block.

eight strips

Step 02

Then sew together two strips. Sew a 3.5 in the white square on both ends. Use the layout below as your guide. Repeat with the last strip of four squares and last two 3.5 in squares.

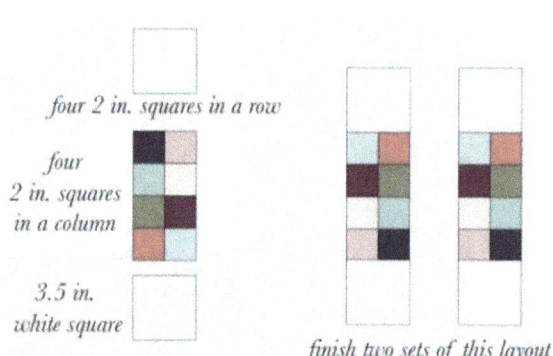

four 2 in. squares in a row

four 2 in. squares in a column

3.5 in. white square

finish two sets of this layout

Step 03

Sew together the two long blocks with white squares on the ends to the 32 square block. Use the layout below as your guide.

Step 04

Place two of your large white triangle pieces on opposite sides of the block. Sew into place and press.

Step 05

Finish off the top by adding the final two large white triangles to the remaining sides of the block. Note: Your white triangles may overhang the middle block. Simply center the triangles to the block.

Step 06

Square off the quilt by trimming it down to the pillow size. If making a mini quilt, square up the mini by making sure all sides are the same length.

Step 07

Finish the mini quilt with backing and binding or finish it as a pillow with backing and piping.

ARROW TABLE RUNNER

Level: intermediate

Seam allowance ¼ in

Finished project size approximately 11.5 in X 37 in

Finished project: a table runner

You can easily make this table runner by adding scrap fabrics to the arrow. This table runner was made to go on my dinette in my 1968 glamper, so it is not as long as a table runner I might put on a long dining table. There is a lot of trimming, so there may be some variation in depending on how generous you are with your cutting.

MATERIALS

- 1/8 yd in 8 fabrics or scraps of fabric
- 3/8 yd White fabric
- 1/2 yd fabric for the backing
- 1/4 yd fabric for binding

CUTTING INSTRUCTIONS

WOF= Width of Fabric

- Four 2.5 in X 4.5 in rectangles in 8 different fabrics
- (see cutting below) *
- Four 4.5 in X 6.5 in White rectangles (see cutting below) *

- Two 3.5 in X WOF white fabric
- One 14 in X WOF for the back (any fabric)
- Three 2.5 in X WOF for the binding (any fabric)

* The 2.5 in x 4.5 in rectangles and the 4.5 in white squares need to have one of their short edges trimmed at a 30-degree angle. Do this by placing a rectangle on your mat and trimming it on the 30-degree diagonal with your rotary cutter. Only do this to one side of each rectangle and square.

BLOCK ASSEMBLY

Step 01

Layout out 16 of the 2.5 in x 4.5 in rectangles with the 30-degree angle on the straight edge. Use the image below to lay out your 16 rectangles. Place one 4.5 in x 6.5 in white rectangle on ends of the rows using the 30-degree angle as a guide.

Repeat this layout as a mirror image to the first row of fabric. Make sure the fabrics are mixed well.

Step 02

Then, sew the two rows together on the angled edge.

Step 03

Trim down the edges with your rotary blade so that the middle arrow is squared off.

Step 04

Sew the 3.5 in x WOF fabric to either side of the middle block. Trim off all the excess white fabric.

Step 05

Finish the table runner with backing and binding

PILLOW PINCUSHION

Finished pincushion: 8″ × 8½″

This oversized pincushion is quite handy. The large size makes it hard to miss when it's time to use it—you don't need to aim, just point your pins in the general direction of the pincushion. The size of the pincushion also makes it hard to lose under piles of fabric.

FABRIC SELECTION

Choose a variety of fabrics for the patchwork. Perhaps highlight scraps from your favorite fabric designer, or celebrate a certain type of print, such as polka dots, as I did here. Try using plaids, stripes, or even a variety of solids.

MATERIALS AND CUTTING

- Small scraps in a variety of colors: each measuring 1¼″–2″ × 2½″
- Batting: 1 square 10″ × 10″
- Pincushion back: 1 piece 8½″ × 9″
- Interfacing: 1 piece 8½″ × 9″ (I prefer Pellon SF101 Shape-Flex.)
- 1 small button for the bottom of the pincushion
- 1 large button for the top of the pincushion
- Embroidery floss or Perle cotton
- Extra-large sewing needle
- Polyfill for stuffing
- Invisible thread for hand stitching

CONSTRUCTION

Step 01

All seam allowances are ¼″ unless otherwise noted.

Sew scraps together side by side until the strip measures 2½″ × 9½″. Press the seams to one side. Trim the strip to 2¼″-wide. Repeat this step to make 5 strips total.

Tip

Use a Short Stitch Length

When sewing snippets, shorten the stitch length on your sewing machine to prevent the small pieces from separating during construction.

Step 02

Arrange the 5 patchwork strips as desired. Sew the strips together. Press the seams to one side. Trim the piece to 8½″ × 9″.

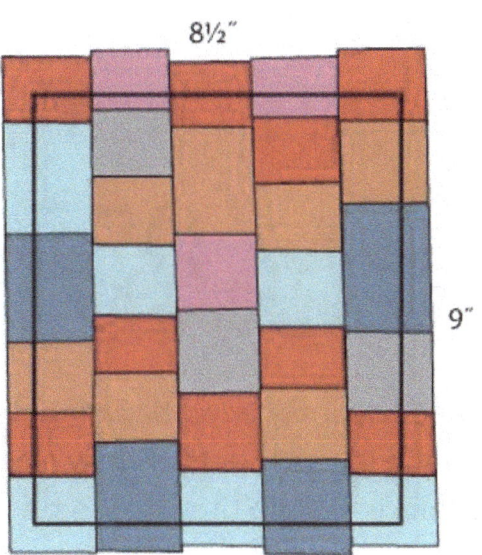

Step 03

Center the piece of patchwork on the square of batting, right side up—a quilt with straight lines close to the edges of the patchwork strips. Then sew around the perimeter of the piece, very close to the outside edge, to hold the raw edges of the patchwork in place. Trim off the excess batting.

Step 04

Fuse the interfacing to the wrong side of the back fabric according to the package directions. Use a pressing cloth to protect your iron.

Step 05

Place the interfaced back fabric and the patchwork piece right sides together. Pin the layers together. Sew around the perimeter, leaving a 2″–3″ gap open for turning—Back Stitch at the beginning and end of the seam.

Step 06

Trim the corners close to the seamline, taking care not to trim through it. Turn right side out. Press.

Step 07

Fill the pincushion with polyfill.

Step 08

Using invisible thread, hand stitch the opening closed with a whipstitch.

Step 09

Use the extra-large sewing needle and the embroidery floss or perle cotton to sew through the middle of the pincushion. Pull the thread tight to compress the middle. Attach a button on each side of the pincushion. Hide the knot and thread ends under the bottom button.

QUILTING FOR BEGINNERS

CHAIN OF DIAMONDS

Finished block: 2˝ × 2˝ • Finished quilt: 50˝ × 60˝

This quilt uses binding triangles: the little corners that are cut off when mitering strips of binding together. The triangles are pieced onto the background blocks in a free-form manner. When the blocks are assembled, the points won't necessarily align, but that is intentional. There is no need to be concerned with precision until it's time to assemble the blocks.

MATERIALS

- White and cream-colored scraps: about 3½ yards total
- 960 binding triangles (see project introduction), or scraps of pink, red, orange, yellow, green, aqua, gray, and black: about ⅓ yard total of each color
- Backing: 3½ yards
- Binding: ⅝ yard
- Cotton batting: 58˝ × 68˝
- Cutting
- WOF = width of fabric
- White And Cream-Colored Scraps
- Cut 750 squares 2½˝ × 2½˝.
- Binding Triangles
- Collect 120 binding triangles in each of the following colors: pink, red, orange, yellow, green, aqua, gray, and black.

or

- Cut 60 squares 2½˝ × 2½˝ in each of the following colors: pink, red, orange, yellow, green, aqua, gray, and black. Cut squares on the diagonal once, yielding 120 triangles.

Tip

Sizes May Vary

Binding widths generally vary from 2″–2½″ wide. For this quilt, I recommend using triangles cut from 2¼″- and 2½″-wide binding strips for the majority of the pieces. Triangles from binding strips that are cut 2″ wide may be used for this quilt, but I would recommend mixing them with the larger-size triangles.

BINDING

Cut 7 strips 2½″ × WOF.

Make It Faster

If you are using a single background fabric for this quilt, cut 9 strips 2½″ × 60½″ and reduce the number of background blocks to 480. Use the 2½″ strips vertically between the columns of pieced blocks.

If you would like to make this quilt but don't want to invest quite as much time as the construction directions require, consider using a larger background block. Start with a 4″ × 4″ or 5″ × 5″ square rather than a 2½″ × 2½″ square. For the colored triangles, use squares up to 1″ smaller than the background block. For example, if you are using a 5″ × 5″ background square, use a 4″ × 4″ square, cut once on the diagonal, for the triangle corners.

FABRIC SELECTION

Various white and cream fabrics were used for the background of this quilt. If you would prefer a cleaner look, use a single fabric for the background. Use a variety of medium and dark values within each strip of color so that the diamonds sparkle. The contrast between the colored strips and the background is important so that the design has maximum impact.

CONSTRUCTION

All seam allowances are ¼″ unless otherwise noted.

Step 01

Place a colored triangle on top of a white background square, right sides together. Before sewing, fold the triangle over the corner to make sure that it will cover the entire corner of the background square. Remember to account for the seam allowance. Sew ¼″ from the diagonal edge of the triangle.

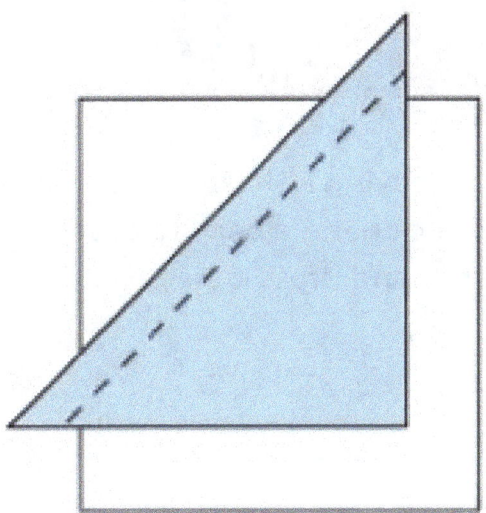

Step 02

Fold the triangle back to cover the corner of the background fabric and press. All of the corner background fabric should be covered by the colored triangle. If some of the background fabric is still visible in the corner, the triangle will need to be repositioned and sewn again.

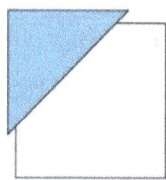

Correct triangle placement

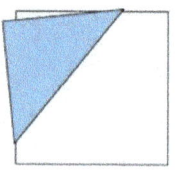

Incorrect triangle placement

Step 03

Trim, leaving a ¼″ seam allowance. Fold the colored triangle back to cover the trimmed corner and press it well.

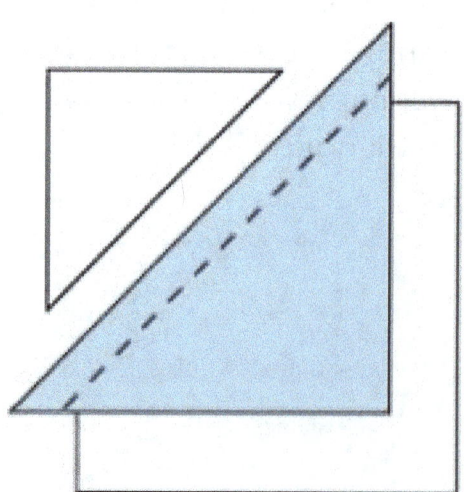

Step 04

Place another colored triangle on the unit from Step 3, right sides together. Double-check the placement to ensure the triangle will cover the entire corner of the background fabric. Sew ¼˝ from the diagonal edge of the triangle.

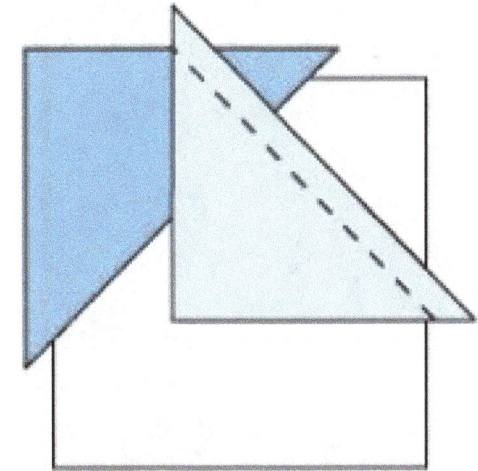

Step 05

Check that the triangle will cover the entire corner and then trim the background fabric from behind the second colored triangle, leaving a ¼˝ seam allowance. Fold the colored triangle back in place and press well. Trim the block to 2½˝ × 2½˝.

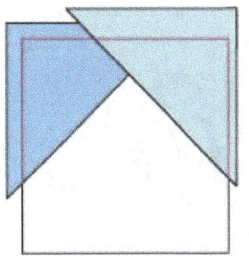
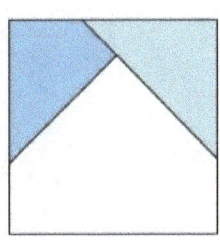

Step 06

Repeat Steps 1–5 to make a total of 60 blocks in each of the colors.

Step 07

Pleasingly arrange the blocks, using the quilt assembly diagram as a guide.

Step 08

Sew the blocks into rows. Follow the arrows for pressing directions. Sew the rows together to complete the quilt top. Press the quilt top well.

Step 09

FINISHING

- Sew around the perimeter of the quilt top ⅛″ from the edge. This will prevent the seams from splitting during handling before it is quilted.

- Piece the back to measure at least 58″ × 68″.

- Baste, quilt, and bind, using your preferred methods. Label if you wish.

- Wash and dry.

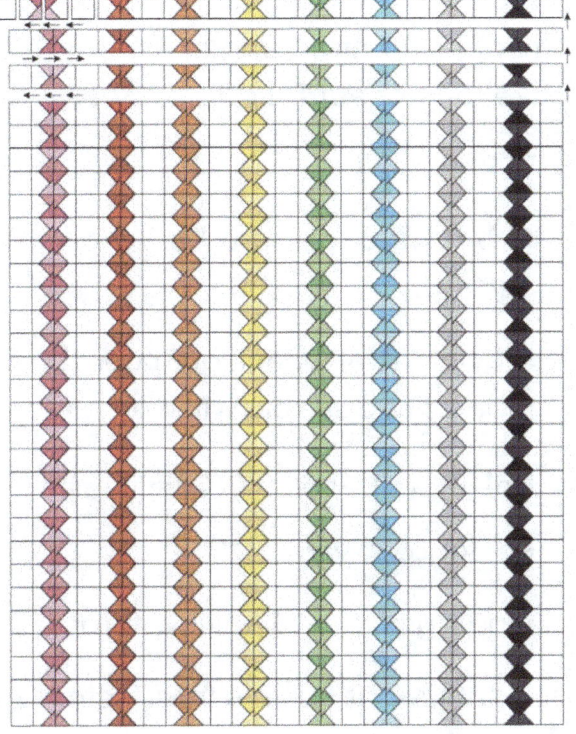

Quilt assembly

PILLOW SHAM

Block Trim Size: 16½″ × 16½″

Finished Pillow: 16″ × 16″

The back of this pillow has an easy envelope closure. The design is made of strips pieced at an angle, using the quilt-as-you-go method. This block would make for a beautiful quilt, as well!

MATERIALS

- Fabric yardages are based on 40″ usable width. Remove selvages before cutting.

- Blocks: ⅓ yard, each of 6 coordinating fabrics for variety. You will have leftover fabric. Fat quarters will work unless you plan to make a pillow larger than 18″.

- Batting: Craft-size prepackaged batting cut 17½″ × 17½″

- Backing: ½ yard

- Findings: 16″ × 16″ pillow form

- Lightweight Fusible Interfacing: 2 rectangles 12″ × 16½″ (optional)

QUILTING FOR BEGINNERS

BLOCK ASSEMBLY

Step 01

Using a ruler and pen, mark a diagonal line across the batting square, as shown. This line will divide the block into an upper half and a lower half.

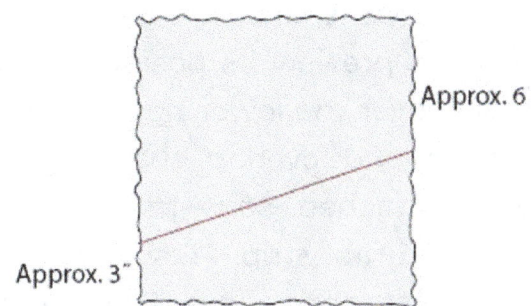

Step 02

Cut a fabric square approximately 9″ × 9″. Align the square on the lower left end of the diagonal line, making sure it covers the lower-left corner of the batting.

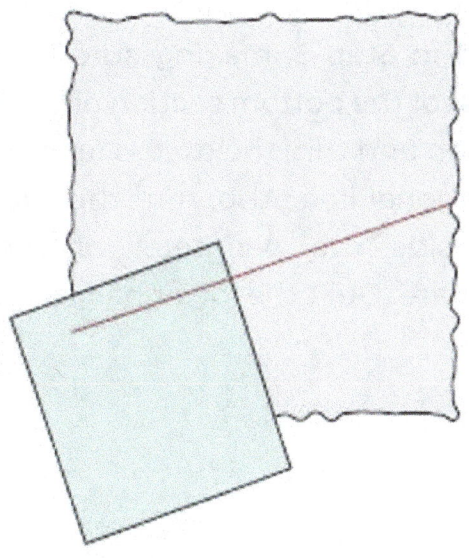

77

Step 03

Cut a strip approximately 9˝ × 13˝. Position it wrong side up at a slight slant to the left so that it fans out. Before sewing it in place, preview its position to see that it will cover the lower right corner of the batting and overlap the diagonal line when attached. Sew—trim excess fabric from the first strip. Press open and trim the excess fabric above the diagonal line.

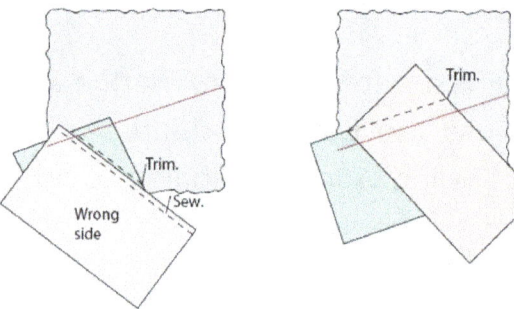

Step 04

Add a strip approximately 9˝ × 11˝ as you did in Step 3, making sure it covers the rest of the bottom section of batting. Press open and trim the excess fabric above the diagonal line. Also, trim the excess fabric outside the perimeter of the batting square. Quilt the lower half as desired.

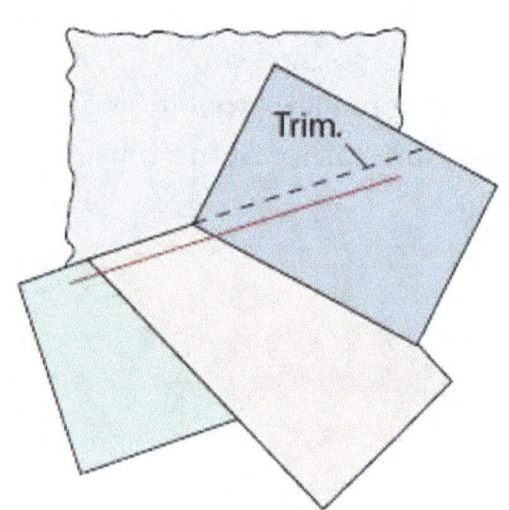

Step 05

To fill the upper half of the batting, cut 3 rectangles approximately 5˝ × 22˝ each. Add a rectangle parallel with the diagonal line. Remember, the diagonal will be covered, so simply eyeball it. Sew and press open.

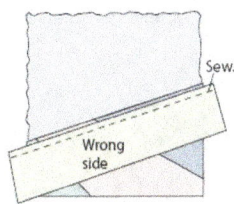 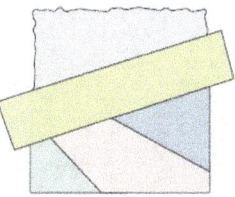

Step 06

Add a second rectangle, previewing its position before sewing to be sure it fans outward and extends beyond the batting at both ends—trim excess fabric from the first rectangle. Press open.

Step 07

Add the last rectangle, positioning it to cover the rest of the batting.

Step 08

11 With the batting side up, trim the excess fabric around the batting square. Quilt the top half as desired.

Step 09

SQUARE UP YOUR BLOCK

Square up the block to 16½˝ using the grid on your cutting mat. Trim a little from 2 adjacent sides of your block to create a 90° angle in the corner of the block. Align the trimmed sides with lines on your cutting mat and trim the other 2 sides.

Step 10

FINISH THE PILLOW

1. From backing fabric, cut 2 rectangles 12″ × 16½″. If you're using cotton fabric and want it to be home decorating weight, iron lightweight interfacing onto both backing rectangles.

2. Turn under ¼″ along a 16½″ edge of both rectangles. Press. Turn under an additional 1″. Press. Topstitch ¼″ from each folded edge on both rectangles.

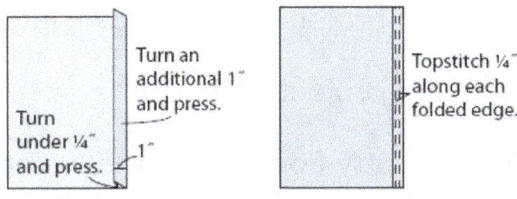

3. With the right sides together, place a backing rectangle on the right side of the pillow cover, with the top-stitched edge at the center of the pillow. Sew around the raw edges, starting and ending with a backstitch. Repeat with the other rectangle on the left side of the pillow.

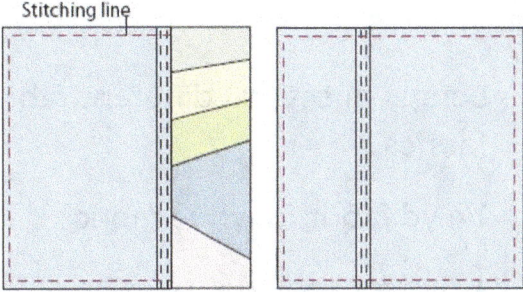

4. Trim the bulky fabric at the corners and turn right side out through the envelope opening. Press.

WINDOW GARDEN MINI QUILT

Level: intermediate

Seam allowance ¼ in

Finished project size approximately 10 in X 12 in

Finished project: mini quilt

These pretty flower pots make the most adorable mini! If you love a little paper piecing, this pattern includes that fun element for you to play with!

MATERIALS

- Scraps of several different fabrics. Please refer to the diagram for choosing fabrics.
- 1/4 yd fabric in white fabric
- 1/2 yd for backing
- 1/4 yd fabric for binding 1/4 yd fabric for binding

CUTTING INSTRUCTIONS

WOF= Width of Fabric

Flowers

- Two different 5 in Square prints (or scraps) for each flower
- One 5 in Square of white fabric

Butterfly

- One 3.5 in Square print
- One 3.5 in Square of white

Pots

- Two different 1.5 in X 4.5 in Prints (pot tops)
- Two different 3.5 in Square prints (pot bottoms)

- One 3.5" x 3.5" in

Other Pieces

- Four 1.5 in X 3.5 in White rectangles
- Two 1 in X 1.5 in White rectangles
- Three 1.5 in X 3.5 in White rectangles
- Two 1.5 in X 12 in White rectangle
- One 3.5 in X 4.5 in White rectangle
- Two 1.25 in X 2.5 in White rectangles
- One 1.5 in X 54 in Piece for single fold binding
- One 14 in X 12 in Backing

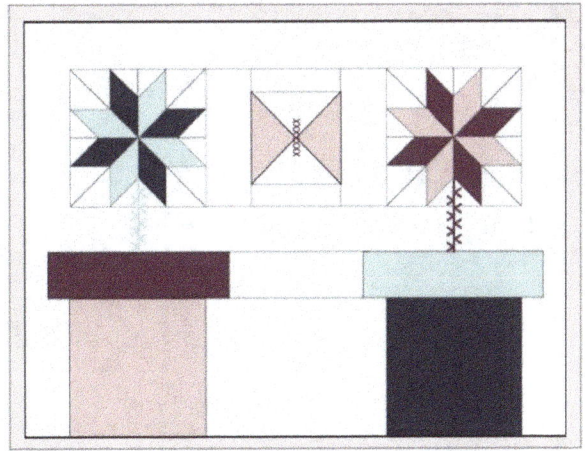

QUILTING FOR BEGINNERS

QUILT ASSEMBLY

Step 01

Sew together the flower blocks using the paper piecing instructions and templates at the end of the pattern.

Step 02

Sew the butterfly block by placing a 3.5 in square of print fabric right side down on a 3.5 in square of white fabric.

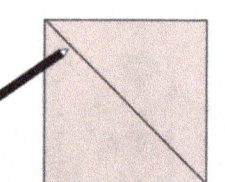
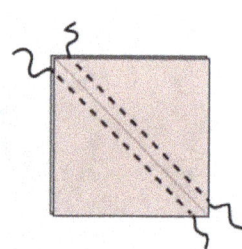

Step 03

Draw a line diagonally down the center of the fabric. Sew a line .25 in from each side of the drawn line.

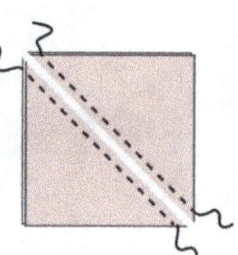
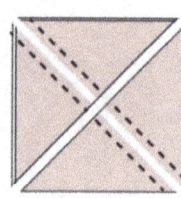

Step 04

Press the seams open, trim off the dog ears, and sew the two pieces together to make the butterfly Press seam open and trim to 2.5 in square.

Step 05

Trim the block down to 2.5 in x 2.5 in

Step 06

Finish the center block by sewing the 1 in x 2.5 in white rectangles to the top and bottom of the center block.

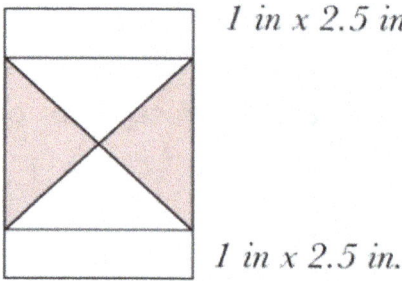

Step 07

Use the diagram to piece together the quilt. Finish rows first then sew those rows together.

Step 08

Use decorative machine or hand stitching to create the stems for the flowers and the center of the butterfly.

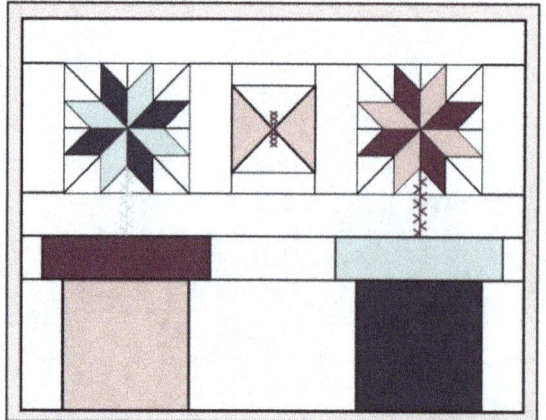

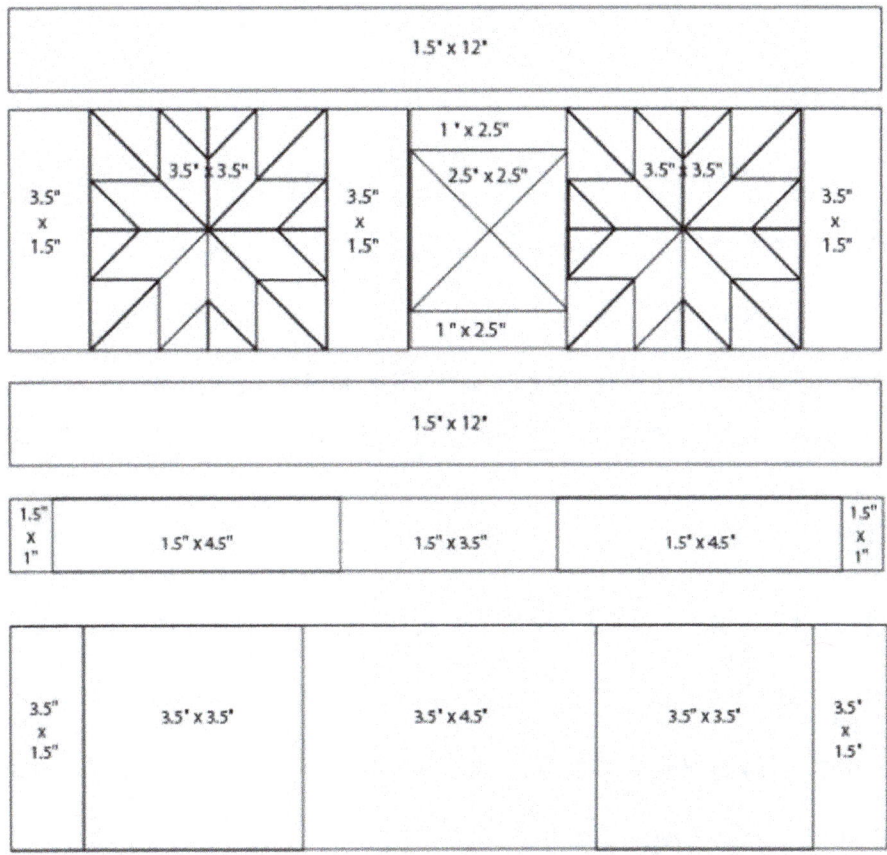

Step 09

Finish the mini quilt with backing and binding.

POSY PATCH MINI QUILT

Level: intermediate

Seam allowance ¼ in

Finished project size approximately 22 in X 22 in

Finished project: mini quilt

This symmetrical mini quilt is so sweet with all its little "flowers in a row." Mary Quite Contrary would be proud! Making the flower is simple and creates a really sweet effect!

MATERIALS

- 5 in Precut (at least 16 squares) plus scraps or extra 5 in Precuts for circles
- 1/2 yd white fabric
- 3/4 yd fabric backing for a quilt
- 1/4 yd fabric for binding
- 1/4 yd lightweight fusible interfacing

CUTTING INSTRUCTIONS

WOF= Width of Fabric

- Sixteen different 5 in Squares cut into quarters (so that their final size is 2.5 in)
- Three 1.5 in x WOF strips of white fabric, then cut this down into twelve 1.5 in X 4.5 in Rectangles and three 1.5 in X 19. in Rectangles
- Two 2 in X WOF in white fabric for borders
- Sixty-one 1 in White squares
- Sixteen 1.5 in In diameter circles with appliqué on the back *
- One 25 in X 25 in Square for backing
- Three 2.5 in X WOF for binding

* Follow the instructions on your lightweight fusible interfacing to adhere the sixteen 1.5 in circles.

BLOCK ASSEMBLY

Step 01

Use a pencil to draw a diagonal line on each 1 in white square (61 in all).

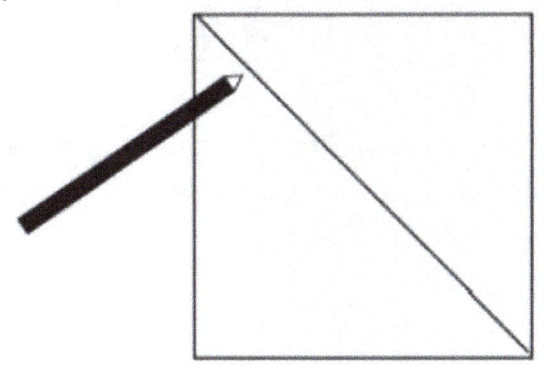

QUILTING FOR BEGINNERS

Step 02

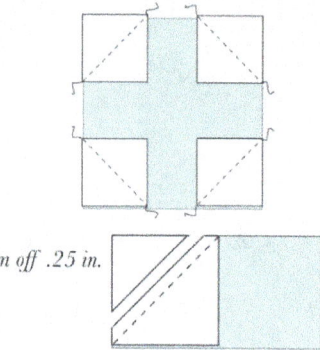

trim off .25 in.

Align a white square in each corner of the 2.5 in square and sew on the diagonal line creating 64 "snowball blocks.". Cut .25 in away from the seam. Press open.

You will have four total snowball blocks from each of sixteen 5 in precuts.

Step 03

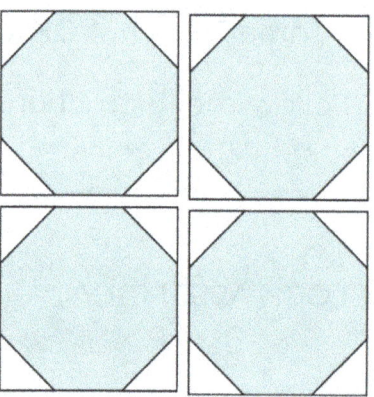

Group the same prints into a four-patch and sew together. Press.

Step 04

Place the appliqué circles in the center of each posy block. Sew the circle as close to the raw edge to secure it into place.

Step 04

QUILT ASSEMBLY

- Layout the sixteen finished posy blocks. Add 1.5 in x 4.5 in white rectangles to the posy blocks and sew into rows (twelve in all).

- Then, sew the sashing between the rows into place. Press.

- Next square up your pillow or mini by measuring two opposite sides. Cut two of the WOF 2 in pieces to the average of the two lengths you measured. Sew into place and press.

- Repeat for the remaining two sides of the block. Sew into place and press.

- Finish the mini quilt with backing and binding.

GIANT HEXIE FLOWER LAP QUILT

It has 7 blocks and an About 41½" x 41½.

Step 01

Join the four pieces with scotch tape. After joining, it carefully traces its image on a sheet. Repeat it till you have hexagons on the poster. Two hexagons ought to be fitted on each 22" x 28" piece of sheet.

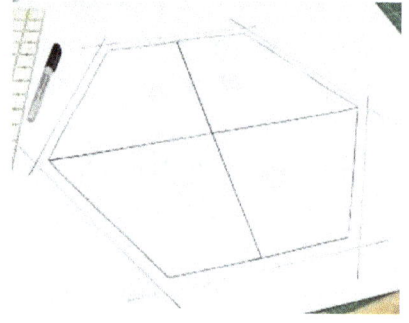

Step 02

Make a fabric pattern. Put your poster made hexagon on fabric and trace it with ½" seam allowance nearby the external edge.

QUILTING FOR BEGINNERS

Step 03

Cut the fabric cautiously from the traced line. And cut out 7 hexagon fabric templates.

Step 04

To lightly paste the poster hexagonal board template on the backside of hexagon fabric, use a glue stick. Place all poster board templates on fabric cautiously so that an even ½" of fabric is perceptible all around the outer corner or edge.

Step 05

After sewing the sides of all the 7 hexagons, then sew your 7 hexagons together in a flower shape. Bind the back and batting with the front, and your quilt is ready.

STAR BABY QUILT

This quilt is completed at the measurement of 41" x 41".

FABRIC:

- 7 Light color 11" x 11" squares
- 7 Colored 11" x 11" squares
- Light 8" x 8" squares
- 18 Strips 3" x 8" and 5 squares 3" x 3" for borders
- 2-yard for backing
- 4/9 Yard for binding

Step 01

On the back of the seven 11" x 11" light color squares, make a diagonal line after that match a colored square with it, and on both sides of the diagonal or transverse line sew a 2" seam down.

Step 02

Using a cutter and ruler, to create 3 half-square trio blocks from each pair, cut five pairs on the drawn line, for 14 half-square trio in total, and toward dark fabric Press the seams. Square up to 10" x 10" for each block.

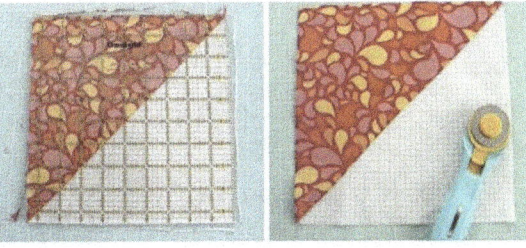

Step 03

In a layout design 10 half-square blocks in a star shape motif with solid light color 10" x 10" blocks in all the four corners that means 5 at the bottom and 5 down. You can use any layout design of your choice as there are many options and variations.

Step 04

Start sewing blocks in six rows, and for each row, press seams in the opposite direction. After it sews six rows and press seams.

Step 05

For the corners sew two sets of four 3" x 8" strips from one end to another. Sew one side of the quilt and press the seams. For the final borders, sew two more sets of four 3" x 8" strips end to end and sew a 3" x 3" square to either end. And sew final borders to the quilt. And the quilt is ready.

QUILTING FOR BEGINNERS

SIMPLY WOVEN QUILT

- The things you will need for this quilt include:
- 3 Jelly Rolls with 38 strips
- 2/6 Yard for binding, any print
- 3" Yard Bella Solid in white
- 80" x 100" for batting
- 1/4 Yards of fabric for a total backing

Step 01

Start and unroll your strips, but keep them half folded together on the opposite sides. Cut the strips according to the following: start by making 26 strips: four 6" and four 10" strips to produce 50g of all sizes. Then cut 26 more strips: five 10" strips to produce 86g overall. Finally, cut 38 strips: four 10" strips to produce 98g in total.

Step 02

From the Bella white solid fabric, cut twelve 10" x WOF, and sub-cut each 10" strip into twelve 5" x 9" strips. It will produce one hundred and two, 5" x 6" rectangles in total. 98 of these are needed.

Step 03

As shown in the image below, take two jelly roll strips of 9" and start sewing four of 2" x 6" Bella white pieces along with the corners of each jelly roll strip.

Step 04

Take the jelly roll strip and swap it straight, or in a horizontal direction, and cut it vertically in half. Make sure that each section measures 4" x 10".

Step 05

Place one long edge piece along the corner of one jelly roll strip of 10", in a different color, which makes it prominent.

Step 06

Measure 3" from one corner of the vertical midpoint, and cut it.

Step 07

Place another strip horizontally equal to the 10" jelly roll strip.

Step 08

Now rotate it and measure 2.5" from one corner of the vertical midpoint of the strip, and cut it off like before.

Step 09

Place another strip horizontally and repeat the same process. Measure 2.25" and cut it off.

Step 10

Repeat the process until there are fifty 14" blocks.

Step 11

By adding the back fabric and batting, your quilt is ready.

DONUTS (THE SIZE OF YOUR HEAD)

Finished block: 18″ × 18″

Finished quilt: 66″ × 90″

There is a bakery in a small town near my house that sells the most amazing donuts—donuts the size of your head! The large-scale blocks in this quilt remind me of those donuts. The interlocking blocks make this quilt look more complex than it is. A design wall is especially helpful when making this quilt because all of the blocks need to be arranged before you begin sewing the quilt top together.

MATERIALS

- Strips and strings in a variety of colors: about 6 yards total
- Background: 2¼ yards
- Backing: 5⅝ yards
- Binding: ¾ yard
- Cotton batting: 74″ × 98″
- 6½″ Easy Angle quilting ruler (highly recommended) or template plastic
- Optional (but recommended): 6½″ × 6½″ square quilting ruler

CUTTING

WOF = width of fabric

STRIPS AND STRINGS

For the squares:

Cut (or collect) approximately 288–360 strings 1½″–2½″ × 7″.

For the triangles:

Cut (or collect) approximately 72 strings 1½″–2½″ × 4½″.

Cut (or collect) approximately 72 strings 1½″–2½″ × 6½″.

Cut (or collect) approximately 72 strings 1½″–2½″ × 10½″.*

*If following Alternative Triangle Construction, you will need approximately 36 strips 3″–4″ × 10½″.

BACKGROUND

Cut 45 squares 6½″ × 6½″.

Cut 12 squares 6⅞″ × 6⅞″.

Sub cut on the diagonal once to create 24 half-square triangles.

BINDING

Cut 9 strips 2½″ × WOF.

FABRIC SELECTION

Strings and strips grouped in color families make this quilt successful. Most of the prints that I used in this quilt are tone-on-tone or mainly one color (plus white). A few multicolored fabrics were used, but sparingly, to maintain the color integrity of each donut.

CONSTRUCTION

Step 01

If you do not have a 6½″ Easy Angle ruler, copy and trace the triangle template onto template plastic. Cut it out with sharp scissors. (Thin cardboard or thick card stock could work in place of template plastic, if necessary.) Or see Alternative Triangle Construction (at left).

Step 02

Sew strings (7″ long) from the same color family together side by side until the block measures at least 6½″ × 7″. Press the seams open or to the side, whichever you prefer. Use spray starch to help the block lie flat. Trim the block to 6½″ × 6½″. Repeat this step to make a total of 4 blocks in the same color family.

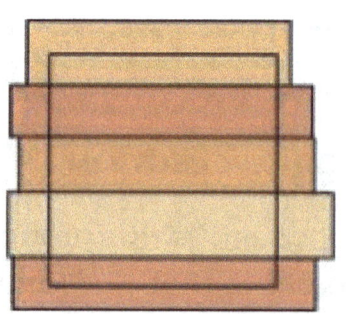

Tip

Vary the Width of the Strips

The number of strips needed for each block will vary depending on the width of each strip. Use wider strips on the outermost edge of each block to allow plenty of room for trimming.

Step 03

Sew strings (4½″, 6½″, and 10½″ long) of the same color family together side by side until the patchwork is larger than the Easy Angle ruler or template. Press the seams to the side. Trim, using the ruler or template as a guide. Repeat this step to make a total of 4 triangles from the same color family.

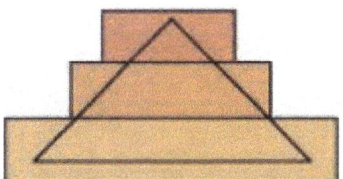

Alternative Triangle Construction

One of the great things about quilting is that there are so many different methods of construction. I used the Easy Angle ruler to make the triangles for my quilt because I had the ruler on hand. The blocks can also be made without a ruler or a template.

Step 01

Start with a 3″–4″ × 10½″ string. This will become the long side of the triangle.

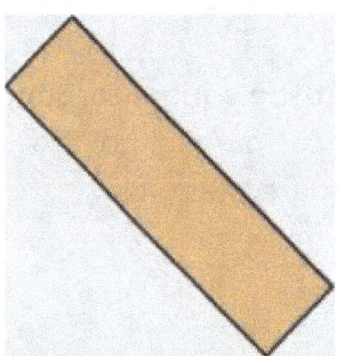

Step 02

Piece shorter strings on either side to make a block at least 7˝ × 7˝ square.

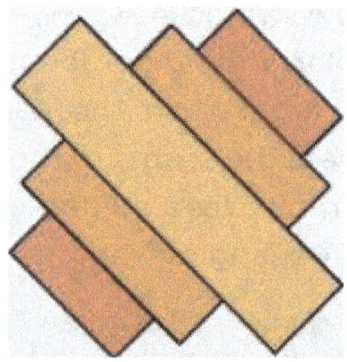

Step 03

Trim the block to 6⅞˝ × 6⅞˝ square.

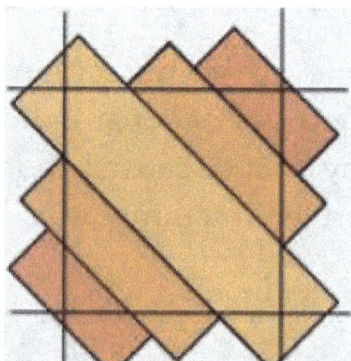

Step 04

Cut the square through the center on the diagonal once, parallel to the seamlines, to create 2 half-square triangles.

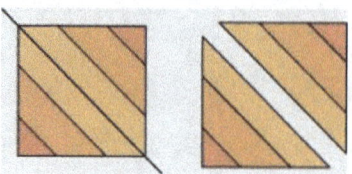

Repeat Steps 1–4 to make 2 string blocks (for a total of 4 half-square triangles) per donut. These blocks will replace the blocks made in Step 3 (at right).

NOTE:

Blocks from Steps 2 and 3 will yield 1 donut when arranged as shown in the quilt assembly diagram (at right).

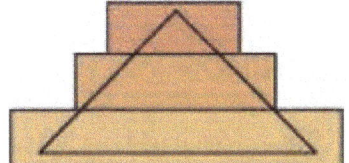

Repeat Steps 2 and 3 to make 18 donuts in a variety of colors.

Place the donut block components in a pleasing arrangement on a design wall. Fill in the background pieces of the quilt, using the quilt assembly diagram (at right) as a guide.

Step 08

Sew the pairs of triangles together to make blocks.

Step 09

Sew all the blocks into rows. Follow the arrows for pressing directions. Sew the rows together to complete the quilt top. Press the quilt top well.

FINISHING

1. Sew around the perimeter of the quilt top ⅛˝ from the edge. This will prevent the seams from splitting during handling before it is quilted.

2. Piece the back to measure at least 74˝ × 98˝.

3. Baste, quilt, and bind, using your preferred methods. Label if you wish. Wash and dry.

SCRAP HAPPY RAILS

Finished block: 12″ × 12″ • Finished quilt: 72″ × 72″

I love a Rail Fence quilt—you can't beat it for simplicity and easy assembly. I thought it would be fun to make super scrappy one, so I started with strings that were about 1¼″–1½″ wide. Charm packs, cut into strips, would work beautifully for this quilt—an easy way to add a large variety of fabrics to a quilt without spending a lot of money.

MATERIALS

- Strips and strings at least 1¼″ wide: about 5 yards total
- Background: 1⅔ yards
- Backing: 4⅝ yards
- Binding: ¾ yard
- Cotton batting: 80″ × 80″

CUTTING

WOF = width of fabric

STRIPS AND STRINGS

Cut (or collect) 900–1,000 strings of fabric that measure 1¼″–1½″ × 4¾″.

BACKGROUND

Cut 12 strips 4½″ × WOF.

Sub cut 36 rectangles 4½″ × 12½″.

BINDING

Cut 9 strips 2½″ × WOF.

Make It Faster

If you prefer a quicker method, this quilt can be made using strip-piecing methods. To do this, use strings that are 14″ long. Piece them together side by side to make a strip set that is 12½″ wide. Press well. Cut the strip set into 3 pieces 4½″ × 12½″. Distribute the strips that are exactly alike into different blocks.

FABRIC SELECTION

For this quilt, I worked with warm colors: pinks, reds, oranges, and yellows. I wanted the quilt to be as bright and cheery as possible, so I chose a fabric with clear white tones only. I refrained from using any fabric that had creamy or gray tones.

CONSTRUCTION

All seam allowances are ¼″ unless otherwise noted.

Step 01

Sew the strings together side by side until the string unit is slightly larger than 4½″ × 12½″. Press the seams to one side. Use steam or spray starch to help the unit lie flat. Trim to 4½″ × 12½″. Make 72 string units..

Tip

Straighten Things Out

If your string unit looks more like an arc than a straight line, you can fix it easily. Add a wedge-shaped piece to either end (or both ends) of the unit. You may need to trim the length of the string unit before adding the end piece(s).

Step 02

Arrange 2 string units and 1 background rectangle, as shown. Sew the pieces together. Press. The block should measure 12½˝ × 12½˝ square. Make 36 blocks.

Step 03

Using the quilt assembly diagram as a guide, pleasingly arrange the blocks, rotating every other block 90°. Sew the blocks into rows. Follow the arrows for pressing directions. Sew the rows together to complete the quilt top. Press the quilt top well.

FINISHING

1. Sew around the perimeter of the quilt top ⅛˝ from the edge. This will prevent the seams from splitting during handling before it is quilted.

2. Piece the back to measure at least 80˝ × 80˝.

3. Baste, quilt, and bind, using your preferred methods. Label if you wish.

4. Wash and dry.

FINISHING

1. Sew around the perimeter of the quilt top ⅛˝ from the edge. This will prevent the seams from splitting during handling before it is quilted.

2. Piece the back to measure at least 80˝ × 80˝.

3. Baste, quilt, and bind, using your preferred methods. Label if you wish.

4. Wash and dry.

Quilt assembly

GARDEN SCENES QUILT

Soft, smudgy colors set off the garden-themed blocks nicely in this delightful quilt. Hand-painted buttons add dimension and texture.

You will need...

- Cream fabric for stitchery background 1/2yd (0.5m)

- Twelve coordinating prints for borders, a fat eighth of each, i.e., 9 in × 21 in (22.9 cm × 53.3 cm)

- Wadding (batting) 36 in (91 cm) square

- Backing fabric 36 in (91 cm) square

- Floral print for binding 71/2 in (19 cm) (width of fabric)

- Hand-painted buttons: one each of birdhouse, watering can, daisy, snail, crow, ladybird, robin, bee, and butterfly

- DMC stranded embroidery cotton (floss): dirty blue (413), soft green (642), dark brown (839), fawn (841), charcoal (844), soft blue (926), and dirty pink (3860)

- Fine-tipped fabric marking pen

- Iron-on stabilizer 18 in (46 cm) (optional)

- Lightbox (optional)

Finished size: 31 in (79 cm) square

Step 01

PREPARING THE BACKGROUND

From the cream stitchery background fabric, cut nine 5½ in (14 cm) squares (one square for each stitchery block). Take the twelve assorted coordinating prints and cut two 4½ in × 3½ in (11.4 cm × 8.9 cm) pieces for border rectangles and five 1 in (2.5 cm) strips (across fabric width) for the Courthouse Steps border around the blocks. From four assorted fabrics, cut one 3½ in (8.9 cm) square, for the corner post squares in the outer border.

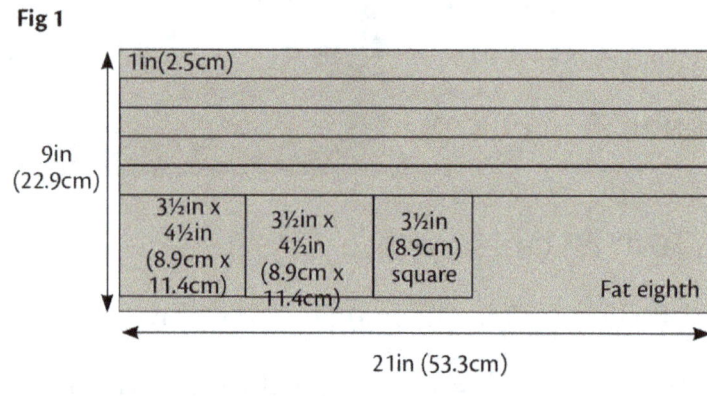

Fig 1

Step 02

BORDERING THE BLOCKS

Each block is bordered by a Courthouse Steps pattern. Take the 1 in (2.5 cm) strips you have cut and re-cut them to produce the following strips.

a – Eighteen 1 in × 5½ in (2.5 cm × 14 cm)

b – Eighteen 1 in × 6½ in (2.5 cm × 16.5 cm)

c – Eighteen 1 in × 6½ in (2.5 cm × 16.5 cm)

d – Eighteen 1 in × 7½ in (2.5 cm × 19 cm)

e – Eighteen 1 in × 7 1/2 in (2.5 cm × 19 cm)

f – Eighteen 1 in × 8 1/2 in (2.5 cm × 21.6 cm).

Using Fig 2 as a guide and 1/4 in (6 mm) seams, sew the strips to each center square, pressing well. Each finished block should measure 8 1/2 in (21.6 cm) square.

Tip

Remember when cutting the strips for the Courthouse Steps border that these are meant to look scrappy. To get this look, I chose my fabrics individually for each block and cut them as they were required.

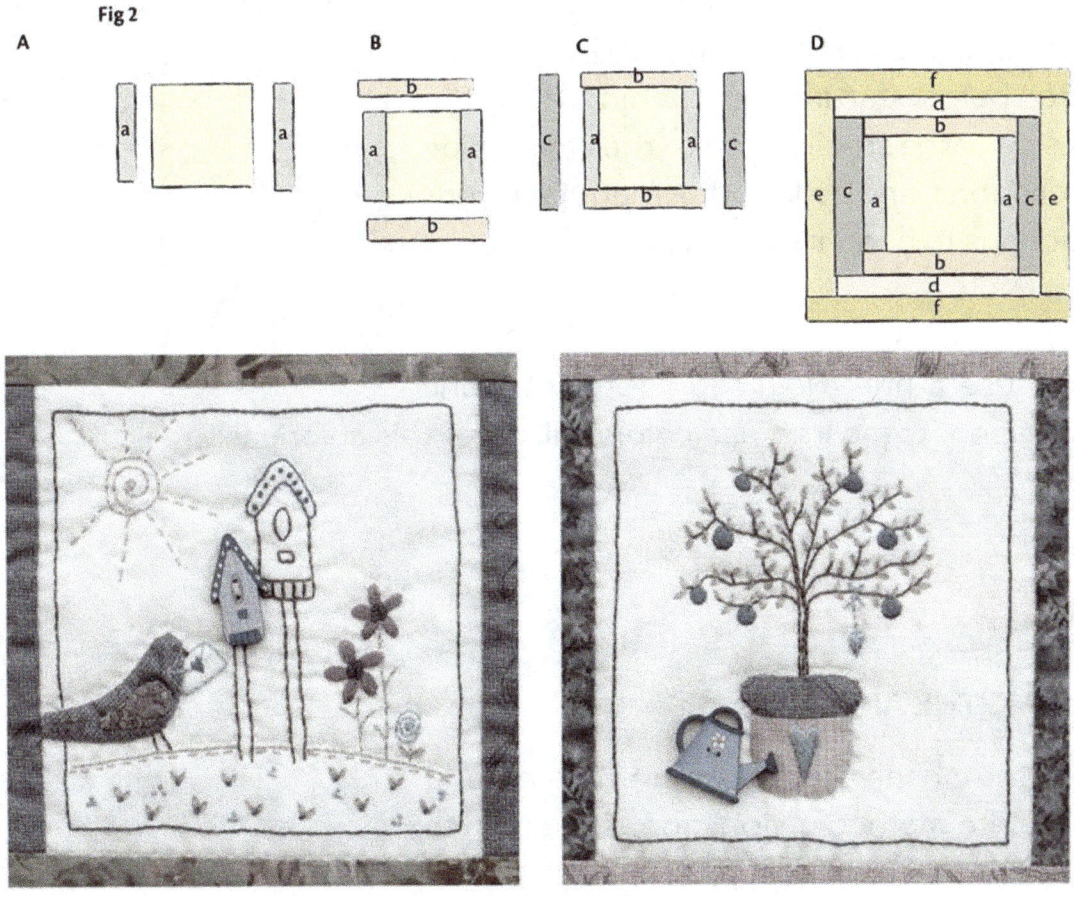

Step 03

TRANSFERRING THE DESIGN

Use the shapes provided in Templates (each block has its own templates). Using a light source such as a lightbox or window, position the center of the block right side up over the pattern and use a fine-tipped fabric marking pen to carefully trace all the stitchery lines. If you are using an iron-on stitchery stabilizer, iron it on before starting the stitching. Place the shiny side of the stabilizer on to the wrong side of your fabric and follow the manufacturer's instructions to bond it in place.

Tip

I like to use a fine (No.1) sepia (brown) fabric marking pen, as most thread colors will cover this color easily.

Step 04

WORKING THE APPLIQUÉ

Apply the shapes using the templates and your favorite method of appliqué. If you plan to use needle-turn appliqué, you will need to add a ¼ in (6 mm) seam allowance to the shapes. If using fusible web appliqué, you will need to reverse the shapes before using it. I used needle-turn appliqué and made templates for the appliqué shapes from paper.

Step 05

Using the pictures throughout the project as a guide, position the appliqué shapes and glue baste or pin the shapes in place. I used a lightbox to help position the shapes and Roxanne's Glue Baste It, which has a nozzle that allows for fine placement of the glue.

Step 06

WORKING THE STITCHERY

Work the stitchery using the stitches and thread colors given with each block template. Use two strands of embroidery thread unless otherwise stated. The stitches used are backstitch (BS), blanket stitch (BKS), French knots (FK), lazy daisy (LD), running stitch (RS), and satin stitch (SS). Numbers correspond to DMC stranded embroidery threads. Once the stitching on all of the blocks has been completed, press your work.

Tip

It is best to sew the buttons in place after the quilting has been finished – see Step 9. Sew them on securely with a matching thread.

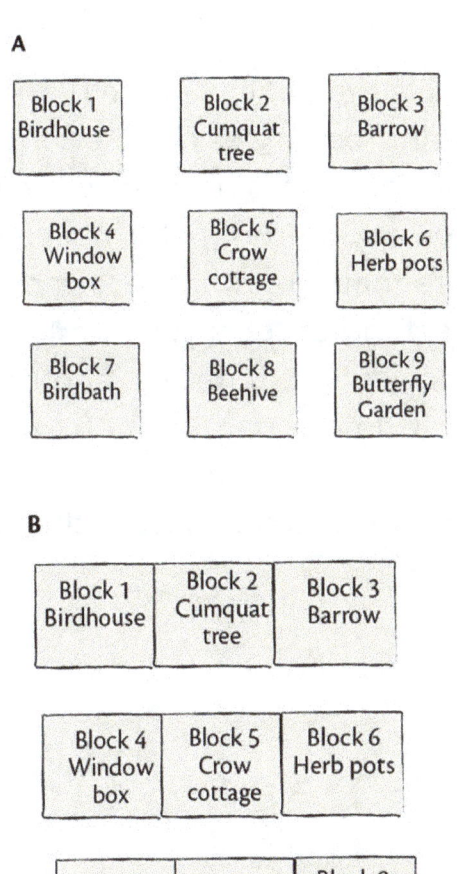

Step 07

JOINING THE BLOCKS

Lay all nine blocks out in order, or order of your choice. Using 1⁄4 in (6 mm) seams, join all the blocks together. First, sew them into three rows of three and then join the rows together, as shown in Fig 3A and B. Press seams well.

Step 08

MAKING THE OUTER BORDER

Take the 3 1⁄2 in × 4 1⁄2 in (11.4 × 8.9 cm) assorted print rectangles cut previously and pleasingly arrange the fabrics. You will need six rectangles for each side of the quilt (Fig 4). Once you are happy with the arrangement, join the rectangles together with 1⁄4 in (6 mm) seams. Now piece together another six rectangles, this time with a 3 1⁄2 in (11.4 cm) square at each end. These strips are for the top and bottom borders. Attach these to the quilt and press the work.

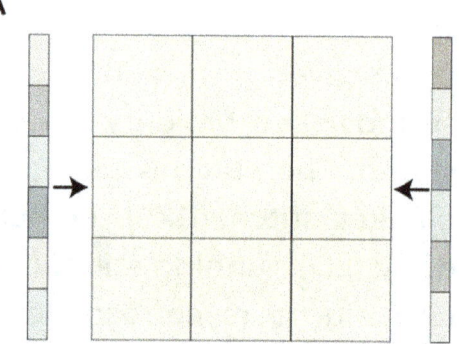

A

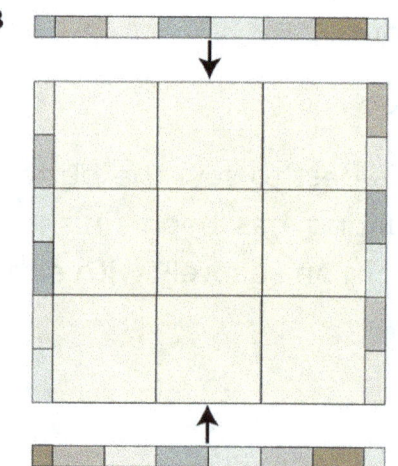

B

Step 09

QUILTING

The quilting uses threads that blend with the fabrics. Echo or contour quilt around each appliqué shape in the blocks. Quilt in the ditch of the seams in the Courthouse Steps border and the outer border. Quilt heart shapes in the outer border, within each fabric piece. Sew all the buttons into position when quilting is complete.

Step 10

BINDING AND FINISHING

To bind the wall hanging, cut a strip of binding fabric 1½ in (3.8 cm) wide × the necessary length (about 130 in (330 cm), on the straight grain. Press in ¼ in (6 mm) down the length. Bind the hanging following the instructions for Binding. Press and then label your quilt to finish, if desired.

CONCLUSION

For beginners, quilting might be very hard and confusing. It will require effort and much of your time to understand fully. You may still find it tough to follow this guide, including the steps in choosing the materials needed for the type of quilt you want to make, the right design for you, and the best approach to planning before you start any quilting project. It's a great idea to educate yourself about common practices and techniques in quilting. Learning on your own is a big contribution to developing your skills in quilting.

If you have made it this far, then it means that you are well intentioned to continue in your quilting mastery journey. There are many ways in which you can increase your knowledge, improve your skills, and become part of a quilting community. You could search and reach out to your local quilting guilds, clubs, join quilting groups on the internet, etc. People who love quilting also love sharing ideas, techniques, and a good dose of fun!

When you feel ready, you might also want to reach out to technical colleges in your area, visit machine repair stores, play a visit to hobby shops or quilt and fabric stores in your area. There you can get in touch with likeminded and experiences quilters, and also check whether they organize regular quilting classes for all levels, including for beginners. But you may be surprised that by then, you might not be a beginner anymore!

The next step is for you to take your skills to the next level by practicing what you have learned. As basic knowledge, ability and practice form the foundation of any skill. Reviewing the materials in this book, coupled with practice, will help you become an excellent quilter.

Good luck on your quilting adventure!

www.ingramcontent.com/pod-product-compliance
Lightning Source LLC
Chambersburg PA
CBHW081402070526
44583CB00020B/2635